Phoenix Rising

Exploring the Astrological Pluto

Haydn Paul

Phoenix Rising

Exploring the Astrological Pluto

Haydn Paul

ELEMENT BOOKS

First published 1988 by
Element Books Limited
Longmead, Shaftesbury, Dorset

Printed and bound in Great Britain
Typeset by Poole Typesetting (Wessex) Ltd, Bournemouth

Cover illustration by David A. Hardy

Cover design by Max Fairbrother

British Library Cataloguing in Publication Data
Phoenix rising: exploring the astrological
Pluto
1. Pluto – Astrological aspects
133.5′3

ISBN 1-85230-042-6

Contents

Beginnings

BY 1905, PERCIVAL LOWELL WAS CONVINCED that there was still one undiscovered planet in our solar system beyond Uranus and Neptune. Using his quite primitive telescope camera and his mathematical skills, he was intent on proving that the orbital variations of these two planets were caused by this new planet, which he thought of as 'Planet X'. Despite his excitement and committed efforts to prove the existence of 'X', he would eventually die in 1916 frustrated by his failure to demonstrate the reality of this hidden planet which he believed was influencing the orbital motions of both Uranus and Neptune. It was to take until early 1930 before a successor, Clyde Tombaugh, was able to provide a clear-sighting and scientific positional data regarding this powerful 'Planet X', during the phase when the planet was transiting through the sign of Cancer.

The mystery planet was soon renamed by the astronomical and scientific community: 'X' became Pluto, a newly rediscovered inner god elevated into the heavens.

Until this century, Pluto had been largely hidden within the unconscious mind of man, revealing its existence through mythology, especially, in the West, that of the Greek and Roman pantheons. Though hidden, Pluto has always had a profound influence on the life of man, but it is only now that man is capable of confronting this energy face to face, as he is offered the choice of life more abundantly or the potential of 'death more abundantly', depending upon which road of transformation he chooses to take. Endings or new beginnings.

The emergence of Pluto in 1930 into the conscious mind of humanity indicates that the time is ripe for mankind to explore a new dimension of life, as a potent new energy with its own peculiar qualities and characteristics begins to have a direct impact upon humanity.

Pluto appears to summarise the challenges facing the world during this twentieth century and beyond, and acts as a directive guide as we pass through the ending phase of the Piscean Age into the incoming Aquarian Age. This is quite appropriate, as Pluto is associated with endings and beginnings, death and rebirth into new life.

In the world of science, Pluto has already been associated with the nuclear industry and nuclear weapons through plutonium, which when used to generate energy or in weapons is extremely powerful, emitting radiation and potential human destructiveness. Initially, this more negative association has been the most obvious, together with a human reaction against the qualities of Pluto which lead to change, and a lack of understanding of the process of which Pluto is the directive guardian. To counteract our potential to create world destruction, Pluto offers the opportunity to create a world transformation, which is an underlying theme in this exploration of Pluto, culminating in the transpersonal vision. An ending or a 'death' seems inevitable in some form; the issue at stake is what kind of new life can emerge, and can it be a triumphal rising of the Phoenix as a resurrection and celebration of life? Or just ashes being blown around the world by the wind?

Individually and collectively, the choice is ours to make. Life is determined by our personal choices, major or minor in all situations, and we have the ability for conscious decision. It is a difficult responsibility, and it is only through an illumination and expansion of consciousness to an inclusive awareness of the self and the world that the right choices will be made. This shift in consciousness is the purpose of Pluto, demanding a great deal from each individual and the collective humanity.

This book is an attempt to clarify and unveil Pluto to the public. It has been written in order to provide a framework within which the necessary shift in consciousness can occur, and to enable the individual to participate consciously in the worldwide process of redemption.

CHAPTER 1

The Pluto Myths

THERE ARE SEVERAL QUITE SUGGESTIVE MYTHS associated with Pluto that reveal some indications and directions towards understanding the nature of the astrological Pluto.

The name Pluto is a Roman appellation and the same character was previously known as Hades by the Greeks, but for both was still the God of the Underworld. Originally the names were associated with the concept of hidden treasures and riches beyond belief, and could only be discovered under the surface of the earth, perhaps approached only through secret caves which slowly descended towards the bowels of the planet, away from the light of the known surface world. This, as interpreted by the Jungian or humanistic astrologer, tends to suggest that the hidden kingdom is that of the personal and collective unconscious mind, where the intrepid traveller and adventurer has to enter alone in order to gain secret knowledge and riches beyond price. Perhaps there can be found the 'pearl of great price', the 'jewel of self' for which all has to be laid on the altar of sacrifice, everything risked in order to gain all.

Hades is today associated with a Western concept of Hell, as a result of centuries of Christian domination and theology, and this is quite regrettable because this connection acts as a psychological barrier to people. Hades, Hell and the lands of the Underworld have been linked to evil and the biblical concept of Satan, and Christianity is always warning against becoming involved with these mysterious realms of life.

It is really a prohibition against contact with the old gods, via the route through the unconscious mind, and tries to prevent individual gnosis being realised in order to maintain the preeminence of Christ and the mediating priesthood. The fact is that the everburning light is found in the deepest darkness, and that 'the path to heaven lies through hell'.

Traditionally, Hades is the land where the shades of the dead are awaiting a rebirth and resurrection, it is a purgatory where a cleansing and purifying process prepares them for the next step on their journey. It is like a limbo, neither here nor there. This is reminiscent of those spiritual teachings that consider man to be asleep, sleepwalking in partial consciousness through life, but believing that he is in fact awake. For the majority of people, the real light is found within the unconscious mind. Thus it is really the superficial mind in which we live our everyday lives that is unconscious; that which we term the unconscious is where the light is to be found. As the Buddha comments, 'the world is upside down'; and 'the light is within the darkness, but the darkness comprehends it not'. If we were not so egocentrically bound, we would consider our conscious mind (a fragment of potential awareness) as truly an unconscious darkness, as we have little understanding of ourselves.

In myths, the light-bringers are often seen to enter Hades or the Underworld, their purpose being to shine their redemptive light to save those tormented souls in purgatory; Christ is one example, during the three days between his death and resurrection. The truth may be that in order to gain their own rebirth they have to discover their own inner light within that realm. Orpheus went to seek his lost soul in the realm of Pluto, descending into the depths of his own nature. Pluto is always a most welcoming host; he does not get to meet very many seekers and is usually engaged in trying to stimulate some reaction from those millions of sleeping shades, and even though the journey to meet him may be extremely difficult and painful, he is waiting to offer the cup that cheers – a heady brew indeed!

Obviously, such myths are allegorical. Gurdjieff suggests to his disciples that man does not naturally have a soul; he has to make or find one. The purpose behind the Master's words is to indicate that considerable effort is required by the aspirant in order to experience the spiritual dimension of life. He is hinting that teachings which declare the 'fact of the soul' may not be true, and can be seen as a temptation to the seeker to try to avoid making a real effort to discover personal truth. Even Gurdjieff's suggestion is not necessarily true, but is really a teaching technique. Where can this elusive soul be found? Within the depths of the inner self: in Pluto's world.

The myth of Persephone displays the fact that Pluto (God of the Unconscious) does not always remain hidden in his own kingdom, but periodically makes an excursion (an away-day visit) into the surface world, to have a poke around and to make his presence felt. Astrologically we could say that he does this by means of transits and progressions.

This is Pluto as rapist, a symbol and image that has most unpleasant associations, especially for all women today, with the apparent increase of sexually violent crimes in Western society. The rise in crimes of a sexual dimension against women and children has connections with the emergence of Pluto during this century and its transit through Scorpio at present. However, the Persephone myth seems to have arisen as a symbolic representation of the process which occurs within consciousness. The story is that Pluto emerges into the light of the surface world, and is smitten by the youthful beauty of the innocent, virginal Persephone, daughter of the nature goddess Demeter/Ceres. The adolescent girl is then kidnapped, taken back into the Underworld, initiated through 'rape' and installed as the Queen of Pluto's kingdom. After a period of time there, Persephone is released, and allowed to see her distraught mother again, but is only allowed a limited time away from being consort to Pluto, and has to return to the Underworld. In some versions, it is suggested that Demeter has to replace her in Hades whilst Persephone experiences the surface world, and this is also tied in with myths of fertility and seasonal rhythms and nature's growth cycles.

Whilst it might appear that this is a tale of evil corruption, it is a symbol for a psychological process whereby the intrusion of Pluto (the unconscious mind) into consciousness is experienced like an intimate inner violation for male and female alike, one that seems impossible to resist or to break free from intact. Often, it has a quality of shock and surprise, certainly uninvited and not welcomed at all. Yet the timing of the abduction is at precisely the point for change to be commenced, where the individual inner pattern of potentiality as indicated by the natal chart is to be stimulated to usher in a new cycle of awareness and expression, a confrontation with 'fate'.

For Persephone, it is the right time to be initiated into her own womanhood, to be forcibly taken away from her previous reality, which is now outgrown, and forced to experience and change to accommodate literally a new world. It is part of a process that has been inevitable from the time of her birth; and as always, Pluto performs the most suitable role of image and symbol as her initiator, or time-keeper of her life. It is an experience which is vital to development, and encapsulates a 'formula' suggesting that a penetration by the unconscious leads to greater light/insight which gives inner integration and self-unfoldment. Persephone emerges from her initiatory 'rape' as a more mature and conscious woman. Gone is the naive adolescent, and she greets her mother again from a perspective of rebirth and greater integration. This process will continue as she returns each year to Pluto's kingdom, because 'a real initiation never ends'; there can be a recognisable point where the process commences, but there is none where it finishes.

Madame Blavatsky's book *The Secret Doctrine* associates Pluto with the attributes of a divine serpent, linking it with the caduceus of the healing profession, and with the serpent and the Tree of Knowledge of Good and Evil. The World Snake, Ouroborus, is associated with the abyss, the chaos from which life emerges, or the collective unconscious from which mind emerges. And it is interesting to note that the original symbol of Scorpio – which in modern astrology is usually said to be ruled by Pluto – was the snake instead of the scorpion. The snake is probably more appropriate than the scorpion, as snakes are able to shed their old skins to emerge 'reborn' with a new outer skin, and this seems a more apt symbol for a sign associated with rebirth.

Pluto is a mysterious and extremely powerful god, and often appears to be shrouded in a cloak of darkness, which can serve well to ward off those who are still unready for his touch, who would shrink in fear from his transformative gaze; and yet the cloak disguises the fact that in the depths of the heart of darkness resides the dazzling brilliance of his light. Pluto is an unorthodox but extremely effective healer of the psyche and initiator of the path of enlightenment, a unifier of contradictory and complementary opposites, a resolver of dualities.

The myth of the legendary bird, the Phoenix, is a surface world image of the hidden reality of Pluto. It is an archetypal symbol of the immortality of the indwelling life within the form. This is the bird that is perpetually capable of being reborn into new life from the fires of the ashes of its old outgrown, outworn self; this is the key to many a human dilemma and to much unnecessary pain and suffering. This exploration is an attempt to turn this key, and to shed some light on the process of working with and trusting Pluto.

If successful, then we can all benefit. Adopt the Phoenix as a directing symbol, use it as a support and guide, and trust in the Phoenix rising.

CHAPTER 2

The Faces of the Astrological Pluto

PLUTO IS ONE OF THE THREE MAJOR transpersonal planets, the others being Uranus and Neptune, all of which have a transcendental quality and which have both an individual and collective function to perform. They can be interpreted as offering a symbolic approach to the process of entering the transpersonal life. With these planets we move from the lightning flash of mind realisation (Uranus), to a mystical heart-felt unity with life (Neptune), to the transformative rebirth and world service which encapsulates the essential changes required (Pluto).

These trans-Saturnian planets symbolise the universal aspects of consciousness, where the mind is operating from a point transcending duality, at a level which is still unrecognised by most of humanity. This means that most people are as yet unable to respond consciously to these energies, and that their impact on humanity is at the level of the collective unconscious – which is why the more 'negative' characteristics seem to be dominant as the energies and inner impulses are not understood or are incorrectly applied. Often, these energies appear to function as inner 'fates', leading blind and unconscious men and women towards situations of crisis, where they feel that their choices were 'inevitable' or that they felt 'driven' to act in certain ways. Ignorance arising from being unconscious of one's inner self is rarely rewarded in life, and more often leads towards greater suffering.

However, an increasing number of people in the world are coming under the direct influence of these planets, and in particular the Pluto energy as ruler of the collective masses and 'disciples'. For such spiritually orientated aspirants, transformation is seen in a world context, not exclusively as a personal redemptive and healing process, but one which is intimately related to service within society as expressed in a multiplicity of ways. For such people, the more that the nature and effect of these energies can be clarified, the greater the possibility that they can be used in a creative and positive manner.

The main themes associated with Pluto concern rebirth and regeneration, the cycle of life–death and renewal, the processes of transformation and elimination within life, and the energy of intrinsic change. These are major themes in life, which in varying ways tend to condition the thinking and dreams of humanity. The development of societies as reflected through politics, religion and culture are responses which arise in reaction to the impact of these themes. Most modern societies are extremely wary of concepts of transformation, rebirth and change emerging within their people. The leadership and political establishment prefer to adopt a reactionary stance designed to impose upon their people a more static social order which gives the illusion of permanence overlaying an often disturbing, chaotic and mysterious world.

The rebirth that Pluto is intimately identified with is primarily focused upon the levels of emotion, mind and self-image or identity. The death and gradual degeneration of the physical form is accepted as inevitable, but Pluto seeks to transform the personal level of consciousness from within. The natural cycle of existence on earth for all life is connected to the passing of time and to the creative power of the universe, which is engaged in an ongoing process of new creation and perpetuating originality, through a recycling of essential creative patterns of form.

As the Pluto energy has a potent expansionary quality, it enters into conflict with those reactionary forces within individuals and society which prefer the apparent stability of the known. Generally, people are suspicious of change, never really trusting that all will work out well in the end. The force of inertia can be constructive in that it slows down the impact of transformative energy, allowing time to adjust to its inevitability; but in the final analysis, it is futile to oppose a universal process.

Most of us are creatures of habit, responding to life along well-worn channels of predictable reactions. When Pluto emerges in our lives, he comes like a shock, casting waves of confusion and destruction in his wake, demanding that we change or face the inevitable consequences of our actions and choices. Our old pattern of self is undermined at its foundations, stability is shaken and those life supports that we have been clinging to are swept away. The hour of rebirth has arrived. Are we ready or able to respond positively? No, we rarely are; and our immediate reaction is generally to attempt to re-establish those old supports again as our protection against the unknown world that has suddenly opened up for us.

Change which is 'forced' upon us and is unavoidable in life is often inwardly associated with our fear of death, triggering that disturbing recognition of the fact of our mortality. The influence of an emerging Pluto stimulates such feelings of unease. Nobody wants to die, and we feel that uncomfortable feeling of impending death trying to force us to look it straight in the eyes. Pluto does not believe in putting new wine in old bottles; the way forward is to destroy in order to renew and re-create a more suitable form to work through, be it an individual or a civilisation.

Often the phenomenon of synchronicity occurs when there are rumblings in the unconscious mind, as 'outer events, people and experiences' are seen (perhaps with hindsight) as strangely linked with inner changes which are happening within the psyche. Some new doors may be opened, whilst other old doors may be closed; relationships can collapse, ideologies become devalued, ambitions destroyed or frustrated. What does become unavoidable is an inner agitation, a shaking free and a dissolving of those habit patterns of attitudes, values, ideals, self-images that we have become hypnotised into believing were ourselves. It is these personality supports that Pluto is determined to transform, stimulating them to a prominence that makes confrontation with them inescapable. These traits are brought to the surface of the conscious mind so that the results of expressing them become obvious; usually, such traits tend to be conditioned by a more selfish tendency, which leads to conflict and lack of respect and right relations with others. Magnified on a world stage, they create global problems.

Attempts at resistance and obstructing this process can be made, but they are likely to create additional distress and suffering. Once unleashed, Pluto is quite ruthless in pursuing its objective, and will disregard those human fears and anxieties as a necessary pain to be suffered on the path towards greater consciousness. Personal panic will only intensify the inner tension, which leads more quickly towards either a breakthrough or a breakdown.

Pluto effects tend to be profoundly cathartic, eliminating outgrown aspects of the self in order for a regeneration to occur.

There is no birth without pain, and in this case, the individual is both the carrier of the new life and the midwife intending to deliver it safely. But the new life is the holder of new insights, a new way of experiencing which will permanently transform the everyday life and world view.

Depending upon the level on which this breakthrough occurs, the change can be sudden and traumatic, like a new world found overnight, or it may take time before the implications of inner change become clearer as a result of personal crisis. At the phase of crisis, one can feel that there are no real supports in life anywhere, that a personal disintegration cannot be avoided, physically or psychologically, and that the ground on which you have anchored your sense of individuality and reality is in truth a quicksand into which you are falling and drowning.

You do not know which way to turn, or what on earth is going on, but you have to endure the process and see it through before its essentially positive nature becomes clear. The first time is the worst because the nature of the process is not understood, and until the peak of the crisis is reached, the underlying meaning is not registered by the conscious mind. Afterwards, you will have a personal insight into the myth of the Phoenix, a symbol for the path of humanity.

Social and intimate relationships are a favourite area of life for Pluto to influence, and here it operates primarily on emotional levels, often focused on basic self-centred interests. Emotions are often the most real experiences of our inner life, and their sometimes hidden ability to be the formative voice in our life choices is often underestimated. Yet it is a dimension of ourselves that is little understood, as its erratic intangibility is hard for the analytical mind to grasp. We are very vulnerable to pain through our emotions, and this suffering can spread across all levels of our being. Most people have a tendency to erect protective barriers around their emotions, inner ones and outer ones, just to prevent a vulnerability to suffering. In so doing, they often deny and repress the potential experience of whole aspects of life, and their emotions find no easy access for liberating expression, eventually forming an inner fermenting poison which can turn them into emotional cripples, or socially dangerous individuals.

Intimacy, and the opening up of protective barriers creates personal vulnerability. Under the possession of that strange experience called falling in love, the inner life disintegrates into a confusing but ecstatic feeling of pain-pleasure. What arises into the life demanding expression, acceptance and integration are powerful desires, passions, needs to possess and devour, an obsession with the loved person, perhaps sexual conflicts, jealousy, even hatred for making one feel so out of control, especially when the other seems so in control and dominant.

This is seen by Pluto as an ideal arena in which to stimulate unconscious activity, to transform areas of inner darkness, through which a passage through hell can lead to a purification and greater wisdom as a result of experiencing the ordeal. Or at least, this is the intention and the ideal of positive growth. Certainly different aspects of the personality emerge as a result of the love process, and often they can be quite shocking to the character that is running amok under the intensity!

Pluto seems to absorb the energy of emotional crisis, using it to fan those flames even higher. It offers the potential of emotional growth and integration usually by the experiencing of the more destructive emotions. The characteristics of possession, obsession and compulsion dominate the individual who is under the unintegrated influence of Pluto, seeming to move him inexorably towards some inevitable fate that is waiting for consummation. The individual can feel powerless to avoid this, or even to have any control over the choice of direction.

Sometimes this can involve the attraction of experiences that are considered to be socially taboo, where the individual feels an intense emotional attraction and repulsion towards his obsessive desires and fantasies. This can be turned into a positive path of illuminating inner darkness, but often this is prevented by the individual's sense of guilt at transgressing social or moral laws. Guilt notwithstanding, Pluto has a tendency to lead people into such directions, partly to act as a liberator for them. In such cases, the pent-up inhibited energy has to be released or expressed in some way; denial or repression only serve to give it extra power. Greater understanding of the nature of these impulses and obsessions can help to bring about a gradual release of the inner pressure and redirect the energy along healthier channels. More often than not, however, the energy explodes into external activity through a temporary state of madness, such as murder or rape and violence.

Remember that Pluto is symbolised as a rapist in the myths. This is no justification for such human actions, but human rape is tied in with the need to dominate (again a negative Pluto quality), and is a reflection of a lack of empathic integration within the alienated and separatist consciousness of the rapist and society. Healing and cleansing the individual will help to heal society.

For one to become free of obsession, there has to be an inner death, a sacrifice. As with Persephone, there is an element of necessary separation and loss, and whether it is love for a person, an ideal or a belief that is given up, the sacrifice has to be something emotionally vital and heartfelt to supply the necessary vitalisation for the transformation. In an archaic sense, it is like spilling one's life blood on the altar.

The natal house position of Pluto is a key to where the archetypal rebirth will begin. At this position, there is a very thin veil between the conscious and unconscious mind, allowing an easy access for Pluto to work through. The sphere of life that this house represents will become quite dominant in the life of the individual, probably as a part that he would like to transform in some way, whilst finding great difficulty in doing so. To achieve this, some change has to occur before obstacles are removed from the path. Whether this is possible or not will depend upon what is required and the ability of the individual to satisfy these requirements. Certainly success may not be easy to gain, yet, once gained, it will have a radical effect upon the life from that point onwards. In that sphere of life Pluto is willing to offer a very important 'gift of integration', but like everything else in life, there is a price to pay.

People in Western society, particularly men, have an uneasy relationship with emotions; in many ways they are considered to be an inferior function, and people are not really encouraged to display their emotions as it is often considered to be a sign of weakness, unless it is within a socially acceptable context. There is no social training for emotional development and understanding as people pass through the stages of life, and it is upon this level that most individual and social problems emerge. The emphasis upon the analytical mind, with its innate divisive tendencies, can create social problems unless tempered by emotional empathy with others; many governments and bureaucracies, dominated as they are by masculine attitudes, adopt policies which are one-sidedly analytical, lacking in emotional empathy. Emotion is a dangerous energy to repress, both on the individual and the collective level.

Social relationships are often ambiguous in nature, and tendencies towards power-seeking and domination can find channels of expression in a social or political context, unmodified by the constraints of the more intimate family relationship. The negative use of Pluto energy manifests more commonly where those unconscious needs to be dominant lead to a manipulation of others in order to achieve purely personal desires. The compulsive urge to gain a position of power over others in order to gain or justify a feeling of superiority over people is a common trait, and one that all of us have surely encountered. Those who are possessed by such needs are self-centred, often unable to compromise and co-operate easily with colleagues, because they are constantly looking for the seat of power. These are driven individuals, almost in the grip of an obsession, attempting to manipulate people and situations so that they can gain personal advantage at the expense of others.

Many people during this twentieth century experience a lack of personal meaning and purpose. Often attempts are made to fill this need by adopting various religious or political doctrines, using them as external crutches to gain a sense of direction in life. This can involve a certain acquiescence to charismatic religious or political leaders, and the attitude of being a 'follower', which is often seen to reflect a need to belong. In some cases this can be beneficial, but such outer supports are always in danger of collapse, especially when the individual finds that such leaders or doctrines are unequal to the task of solving those problems which they claim to be able to solve. The price of disillusionment can be high, and can have a negative impact on those who have mistakenly invested too much of themselves in fulfilling a role as follower, only to find that their world comes crashing down upon them – the world in which they had such a naive faith and trust.

Humanistic and transpersonal astrology is concerned with the individual's search for meaning, but its real emphasis is upon discovering this meaning within the self, and not having to rely upon outer supports which will inevitably collapse. This inner meaning, which is experienced as a strength, a feeling of security and stability, intuition and direct knowing, is an intensely personal world, almost operating under its own laws and principles. It is the world in which one awakes who has achieved a transpersonal crossing.

Whilst Pluto is known as the Lord of the Underworld, it seems that his main purpose is to empty his kingdom, to release the contents of the unconscious mind into the light of consciousness. This is a perpetual, ages-long task, almost like the futile attempts of Sisyphus pushing the rock to the top of the hill, only to see it roll back again. Yet Pluto knows that his efforts do reap some results, and that the energy is certainly not wasted and there is some permanent development.

To enter into this world of meaning requires considerable faith and trust in the benign intention of the universal life. Unfortunately, most people do not have a sufficient trust, even those who profess a belief in a pure and good God. At its highest point, Pluto issues an invitation which is an offer to experience union with 'God'; most people instinctively turn away, refusing to accept the invitation, pleading that they have prior engagements to fulfil. Often, these include giving lectures on 'spiritual teachings', or else going off on those weekends in country houses listening to those lectures. After all, one must get one's priorities straight!

Pluto manipulates events in order to encourage (force) a person to face his own nature, be it a hidden self or the way he expresses himself within social and intimate relationships. When it is in aspect to a personal planet, either natally or via transit, it indicates that some light is needed in the sphere of life associated with that planet. A rebirth is demanded, and part of the unconscious requires redemption or a latent quality/talent needs expression. These areas hold keys to an amplification of meaning and purpose in life, and should be seriously explored and worked with. This is the aim of a positive response to Pluto.

There is a tendency for Pluto to stimulate the forming of a particularly difficult problem or challenge for the individual. This takes the shape of an obstacle, a barrier to real progress, and yet is also a summation of that individual's development to that point. Often, the form that this obstacle takes is related to Pluto's natal house position. It is a confrontation with frustrated desire, a desire that seems to absorb much of the energy of the conscious mind. This desire is one that is essentially within the scope of the individual to satisfy or resolve, and yet efforts to do so are constrained, perhaps by environmental reasons such as family or economic considerations. Yet the frustration intensifies, vitalising the obstacle even more. It often seems like a brick wall that one is confronting; one is forced into a direct encounter with these living compulsions, unsatisfied passions, where the sheer impossibility of ignoring their reality has to be acknowledged. It is a blockage of energy, yet it can seem like a black hole into which aims and objectives pour and circulate around in search of an answer, a way to heal what feels like a festering wound in the centre of your mind and heart. It is reminiscent of the wound of the Maimed King of the Wasteland in the Grail Mystery tradition, who can never be healed until the successful Grail Knight arrives with the answer or solution which resolves the nature of the tormenting problem. The individual has to become his own Grail Knight. The renewal of the individual (or the Wasteland) through finding a way to release the vitality of the wellsprings of life must occur to stimulate the healing process.

Similarly, it is reminiscent of the technique of the Zen koan, where the Master gives the aspirant a question, to which the aspirant is expected to demonstrate his understanding and insight. The problem is that this question cannot be resolved or answered by the analytical conscious mind; the Master is attempting to stimulate in the aspirant a direct, unconditioned experience arising from intense efforts devoted to 'answering the question'. Essentially the mind has to be broken/transcended in the process of meditation and obsession by the koan (obstacle). A typical koan is 'If you are not enlightened in this life, then in which life do you propose to be?'

The obstacle is a gateway to a new fertile land, but Pluto demands some form of inner death and sacrifice to pay the gatekeeper, and the cost is high but so are the rewards. Certainly, once the obstacle reaches a certain 'size', it is essential for the personal well-being to deflate and resolve it; otherwise it will cast a very long shadow over the whole life, poisoning and spoiling it in various ways. The door is there, it is always open, yet the problem may lie in the fact that you are standing looking at your own shadow which appears to be much larger than the door, and so you believe that you cannot progress and pass through the exit-entrance to a new way. Or perhaps the door is closed, and you are pulling it instead of reading the instructions to push.

In astrology, Pluto is usually considered to be a 'feminine planet', and whilst this does have some relevance, I consider it to be a limiting perception, in that 'feminine' is much too restrictive, especially in the way that our minds are likely to interpret it. Equally, to consider it to be bisexual, androgynous or even masculine does not reveal its real nature, because depending upon the approach made it is quite capable of reflecting all these facets to an explorer. What it appears to be is a reflector of an archetype of unity behind all those expressions of sexual dualism and opposites that we experience on earth. Transcendental or cosmic 'sexuality', a point of ecstatic resolution, or a seed of the human being, essentially neither male nor female. The Eastern symbol of the Tao appears to be an apt representation of the peculiar energy of Pluto as experienced by humanity. Containing the inner dualism of the Yin and Yang as symbols of the world of opposites, and yet resolved within the holistic circle of the Tao.

Yet for the individual, Pluto has a masculine, aggressive, penetrative approach, forcing a response of 'feminine receptivity' regardless of the physical sex of the person. Pluto has been linked with the Divine Feminine, reflecting the images of Great Mother, Goddess, Kali, but this does not necessarily mean that it is a rebirth of an archaic feminine power prefiguring a new age of 'Woman'. Certainly Pluto works particularly on the emotional level, as a counterweight to the current overdominance of the analytical mind in the West, but its influence is powerful on every level. What I feel it preshadows is the dawning of an age of Humanity, of the Human Being as a holistic entity rather than as its separated sexual forms. In that sense we are ready to begin moving beyond the Yin and the Yang into a conscious experiencing of the Tao.

This stimulation of enhanced world feeling will lead to intuitive empathy and a coming together of both mind and feelings into a new, integrated being. It is towards a balance that the emphasis is directed at present, as polar opposites can be dangerous extremes. The rising of the women's movement and emancipation in the West is a sign of a balance being adjusted, preparatory to new progress. The birth of a new consciousness needs to be viewed from a perception of unity and synthesis, not from any attempt to re-elevate any of the conflicting opposites into a dominant position. That time has passed.

Pluto is no more opposed to patriarchal structures and systems than to matriarchal ones. He subverts them all when the cycle is ending naturally, because all have failed in some way to act as suitable forms of expression for evolutionary progress. What is needed is a new foundation and structure suitable for the future, and that will be considered in Chapter 8.

Pluto is associated with the Hindu trinity of Brahman, Vishnu and Shiva, which represent the three main energies of creation, preservation and destruction respectively. The disguise is that of Shiva, Lord of the Dance, the Great Destroyer of Worlds, which is needed so that the great creative fecundity of Brahman can recreate even more impressive universes. Pluto is like a great cosmic seed which always holds the potential for greater life; to enter into receptive consciousness and relationship with this energy gives the individual the power of perpetual renewal and growth.

CHAPTER 3

God of the Underworld

CONTEMPORARY HUMANISTIC ASTROLOGY has emerged in recent years displaying a revitalised relevancy for the modern world, which is mainly the result of the merging of twentieth-century psychology with the essential myths and images of astrology. The coming together of Jungian psychology and astrological insight and symbolism, plus the increasing need of individuals to discover their own inner connection to enhanced meaning, purpose and direction in their lives, has created the new person-centred astrology. This form of 'objective' reflecting centred on the natal chart data, can offer new modes of self-perception and indicate those inner patterns which offer the development of personal potential, or ways to resolve inner problem areas, as well as insights into how the individual can use his life energies in a responsible and beneficial manner. It is concerned with the need for personal wholeness and integration of body, emotions, mind and soul, to create a state of inner balance and well-being. As the world is a reflection of the state of humanity, then as Jung suggests, if there is something wrong with the state of society, then there is something wrong with the state of the individuals who comprise that society. Each of us is a contributor and participant in the world; by our own actions, deeds, thoughts and emotions we have a real influence, locally and collectively. Thus we cannot deny our share of world responsibility; we are all responsible.

Whilst many people would like to mould the whole outer world to fit their own personal preferences and prejudices, it is not that simple. It appears that there is an underlying pattern which is directing the overall evolution of the world, a vast planetary consciousness, which recently has been termed 'Gaia', and in esoteric spheres is 'Sanat Kumara, The Ancient of Days'.

Although it may seem that powerful individuals can have considerable planetary impact, if their attempts at influencing the planetary direction are not aligned with the hidden purpose, then they inevitably fail and are consigned to history. Humans can be presumptuous in their arrogance, challenging the gods with an overabundance of hubris.

The point is that real change can only occur when it is in harmony with the inner nature of things, human or planetary, and integration involves the transformative acceptance of things as they are, and within their own innate directive patterns of purpose. To create the potential for world change, we must each become transformed so that we begin to embody our own unique pattern of being, which at its essence, corresponds to the hidden planetary purpose.

Both Jungian psychology and humanistic astrology are ways of attempting to lead people towards personal integration and wholeness. Greater understanding of those hidden inner processes at work within the human being can be gained, and co-operation with inner movements for change can be made. Prior to looking more closely at those aspects of the Jungian approach which are especially relevant to understanding how Pluto operates, it can be constructive to consider the nature of wholeness.

WHOLENESS

The human being is a unified organism; the automatic self-regulating mechanism of the physical body is a wonder in itself, and is the 'temple for our being'. Our vehicle of manifestation on earth is physical-etheric, emotional, mental and spiritual. In most contemporary mainstream psychology, we find that the reality of the transpersonal dimension ('spiritual') is taken into due regard as a truly essential aspect of the whole person. However, the problem for all of us lies in the inescapable fact that, within consciousness, we are all somewhat fragmented, not fully centred, out-of-phase and often quite unbalanced; and here I am considering the state of what is commonly perceived as the 'normal, sane, adjusted member of society'. Do you ever look at events in the world, and wonder if they are the product of a 'sane society'? It has been said, humorously, that the 'Earth is the insane asylum of the solar system'; it can certainly be a painful planet to live on. But let us hope that enough people aim to find real sanity and balance, that of individual wholeness, because our society cannot be whole and healthy unless we are. So we strive towards personal integration, and it is not easy. As Jung states, 'there is no coming into greater consciousness without pain.' It can be hard, prolonged, painful self-exploration, seemingly never-ending, often apparently non-productive, but you will, in time, come together, and the fiery joyous intensity of the Self will pervade your life, like a descent of grace, a blessing.

Obviously, the path to wholeness will vary from one person to another, but there are several aspects of the process which are common to all. From birth, we are heavily conditioned by society, via parents, school, religion, education, governments, in order that to become members of society we should think, feel and act in certain predictable, limited ways. Conformity is the key, and is rewarded by social leaders; non-conformity is penalised in various ways, depending upon the attitude of the particular society. Some of this can be quite necessary and productive for the growing child, but some can be detrimental or even destructive to the evolving being. A child's mind and heart are wide open to all influences, and whatever goes in will act as a deep programme affecting the remainder of the life, producing an almost robotic set of responses and reactions.

Relationships with parents are likely to colour future adult relations with the opposite sex, or with one's own sex. Often, those who have spent considerable time seeking self-unfoldment discover a vast amount of hidden conditioning which they have been 'playing out' in situations evoked by everyday life in a quite unconscious and automatic reaction, and have believed it to be their 'real self'— but is it? Such conditioning can be in the form of religious dogma unfounded on personal experience; life attitudes/purposes (good job, lots of money, big house, big car, etc.); or morals ('you should live like this', 'good boys and girls don't do things like that', 'homosexuality is evil and sick', etc.).

Take a look at yourself; do you really think all these things? Are they really your thoughts and emotions, or have you been almost hypnotised into believing that you see life that way, by the non-stop social programming transmission?

Often the search for a more real 'self' commences when a person begins to realise that they do not know who they are, and wonder if they still exist when the perpetual inner programming is taken away. Our way of experiencing and looking at the world is almost inherently prejudiced and flawed, and it is as though we have a thousand heads on top of our own, all speaking at different times through us, like ventriloquists. Often people wake up to realise that the life they have been living is the result of parental or societal wish-fulfilment.

In Zen there is the experience of *satori*, the state of the 'unconditioned mind', where like a shocking lightning flash, the mind's conditioning collapses and for the first time we consciously experience our self and the world without veils and programmes. A Zen koan seeks to cut through this knot of conditioning: 'What was your original face before your parents were born?' So, whose life are you living, and how strongly conditioned is it? Is it a free life?

Wholeness is not 'perfection'. The human being is perceived as a fusion between 'animal and the divine', and as 'light' is not all light or all darkness, but a living, changing relationship between the two, so are we. Integration is a result of a process of redemptive cleansing, of releasing all the inner rubbish that is blocking our awareness of our own inner light.

But we do not wish to be like a saint who has repressed all his own 'lower desires' as impure, and alien to his own created image of 'spirituality', and then becomes so afraid that the dam walls will burst, revealing him as only a plaster saint. To be whole is to be more like a 'sage', one who accepts the totality of his own nature, sees life as it is, sometimes painful, sometimes joyous, accepts his own inevitable death, lives by his own light, and tastes life fully.

Finding the hidden self always involves the stripping away of the multiplicity of partial or false selves, images and supports in order to release the natural being. Psychologically, many adults are still children, and refuse to face the lessons that life confronts them with, preferring to do a 'patching job', just enough to alleviate the immediate problem, so that they can feel a bit easier for a while, kid themselves that they've solved the problem and carry on—until the same set of problems arise again and they are back to square one. If we find that the same problems reoccur, that appears to demonstrate that they were never fully resolved in the first place.

It is better to face such problems, and to enter into the darkness and pain of them, moving deeper towards the heart of the suffering, and in due course, the darkness becomes transformed into light and the problem aspect has been released and redeemed, and should not reoccur, at least on that level of the spiral of life.

This is like the journey of Orpheus into the realm of Pluto, god of the Underworld, in search of his lost soul.

Basic problems, which are often emotionally charged, cannot be solved on the level on which they emerge. Hercules found that fighting the Hydra on its own terms, on its own level, was self-defeating. By translating the problem to a higher level, however (by raising the Hydra above the ground), the problem became immediately capable of resolution. All forms of separatist and dualistic conflicting relationships need to be raised to a non-dualistic level in this way, to enable us to perceive the solution.

Most people find it difficult to live with themselves; fragmented and contradictory voices jostle for power and influence within them, because there is no true centre established, apart from the social ego with its multiple 'I'. People cannot accept and love themselves, all of themselves, in the fullness of their own nature. Most like some parts of themselves, disliking, evading and ignoring other parts, because they do not fit into some idealised self-image that they choose to see themselves as, and this is a personal creation masquerading as a 'self'. This is a prime way to create inner difficulties, taking the person away from a potential harmony and wholeness into psychological 'dis-ease'. Nobody is perfect, but we often seem to feel guilty when we aren't, and condemn ourselves and others for being, after all, just human.

Our illusions and expectations of others are a problem, and conflict is caused by anger at the disappointment of shattered illusions. It is essential to learn how to love yourself, accepting yourself in every aspect; even those 'negative' aspects will change through the power of such real acceptance, because it is a way of cleansing your own Augean Stables of ancient muck and rejection. If you can do that, you will be able to accept others more readily, have more satisfying relationships, and take a vital step towards integration.

Full self-responsibility for our own lives is essential; it appears to be a natural process that everything we experience we attract to ourselves, and that events do not happen to a person, but that he happens to them. He confronts them, giving his own sense of meaning to his experienced encounter. Often, much occurs in life that is hard to understand at the time, yet with hindsight, we can see meaning and hidden purpose in our experience. One way of relating to the world is to assume full responsibility for all we experience. Our reactions, actions, thoughts, feelings, emotions and the interplay between our inner processes (which may occur without conscious choice or volition) and the 'outer world' combine to unfold our lives. As Madame Blavatsky says in *The Secret Doctrine*, the universe is unfolded and guided from within outwards, and so is our path through life; others may influence and affect us, but our reactions to outer stimuli are our own responsibility.

In every situation and experience in our dualistic world, there is a dynamic process occurring wherein both 'opposites' interpenetrate and transform each other. This implies that just as the planets are Janus-faced, expressing energy that is both positive and negative, no experience is either exclusively 'good' or 'bad','constructive or destructive', 'light or dark', etc. Everything interpenetrates everything else, forming a flowing intrinsic unity. The seeker may find it useful to cultivate a state of consciousness wherein what changes is just the proportion in which the opposites relate, a 'more-or-less' instead of the analytical mind's 'either-or'. Any experience which is perceived by the mind as 'good or bad' can create a deep split leading to inner conflict as the mind pursues only the arbitrary 'good', denying the 'bad', which then sinks into the unconscious mind. It may be wiser and more positive to regard experiences as a combination of more light and less darkness, or vice versa; this offers a perceptual standpoint that can give a more whole vision of the interacting forces within any partial experience, and thus function as a creator of meaning in life, because meaning emerges into the light of consciousness only through awareness of greater patterns of holistic existence.

Wholeness is a way towards freedom from a limiting, false, partial self, a self that is outgrown. We have to acknowledge that our psychological state, individual and collective, really needs a deep cleansing and healing. We need to resolve that dichotomy of conflict which we have all experienced between 'head and heart', mind and feeling. If this can be achieved, it leads to a great inner unification, vital for everyone, and will reflect the state of consciousness indicated by the esoteric statement 'As a man thinketh in his heart, so is he'. Wholeness implies a psychological unity, a focused totality of the being, where the individual has achieved an integration and clarity, and is fulfilling his innate pattern of 'destiny' as preshadowed by the natal horoscope.

This is the hidden purpose of Pluto, to aid in the creation of planetary wholeness, through the individual and society. Dispassionately, it stimulates all unpurified aspects within its subjects so that the potential is there for conscious acceptance and refining of the inner dross through the fires of transformation. It has little interest in judging, and is concerned with just accepting whatever is found as a preparatory step towards using it for individual growth, which in turn is part of planetary healing.

ARCHETYPES AND THE UNCONSCIOUS MIND

The human mind, has a series of inhibitory 'filters' or 'veils', some evolutionary and some merely social, which control the amount of information being received by the brain via the nervous system and our physical senses. This information is converted into a personal experience of ourselves, the world and reality; and the potential of each life is restricted by those filters that are partly created or exaggerated by whatever type of social conditioning and programming we have undergone during our formative years. These make up the fundamental world view or paradigm that becomes a consensus social reality, which all members of a particular society are then expected to support and maintain in continuity.

It is obvious that we only consciously experience a fragment of reality, that part of it which we can cope with and are able to impose a 'stable human reality' upon. It has been said that too much reality is too much for the human mind to bear, and this is true, especially when the human mind is attemping to hold onto its limited world view of partial reality when confronted with a much more inclusive experience of it. Then it is a dangerous and shattering encounter, and a mind that cannot cope with the new dimension that is opening up before it may lapse into madness. However, if the mind's programming is released and dissolves, then an expanded consciousness emerges which is capable of permanently embracing a larger reality whilst still being able to function within the social consensus reality. This is the initiate, who has opened the inner door to allow his unconscious mind to be illuminated, and thus made conscious.

The unconscious mind is the repository of all that we are not fully conscious of, whether it is personal memories or species blueprints, aspects of self that we prefer to repress for personal or social reasons, but it is not just a dumping ground. Within the unconscious mind is the personal unconscious, a collective one, and what may be termed a superconsciousness. The unconscious levels are the inner realm of the archetypes and the gods, and it is

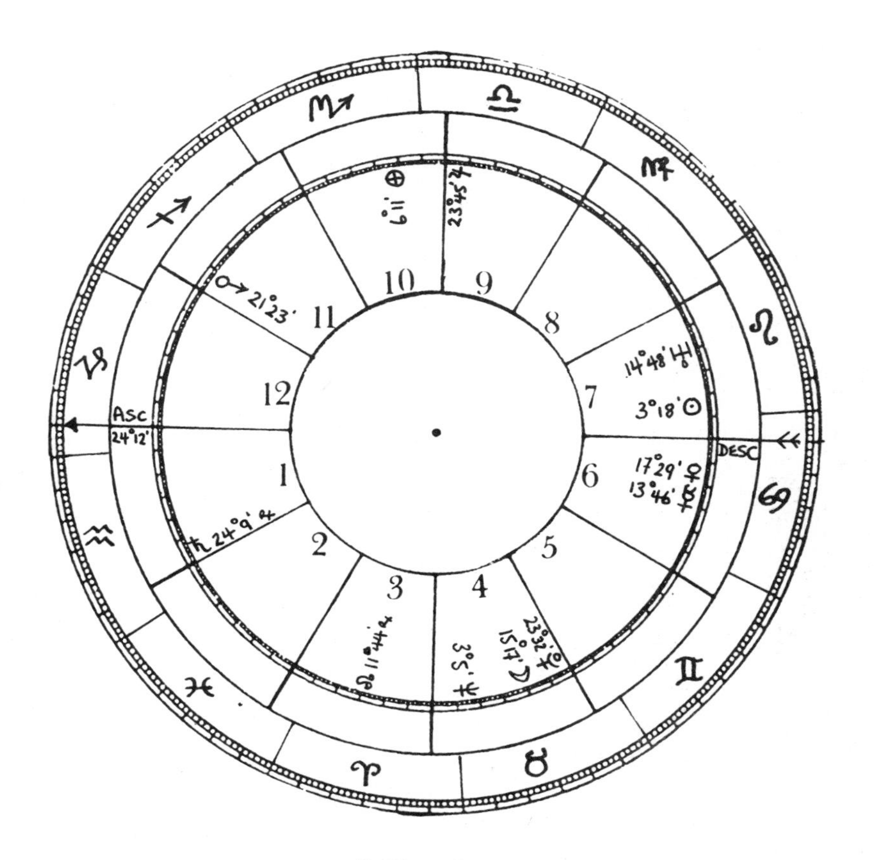

Carl Gustav Jung
Psychologist,
Explorer of the
unconscious mind
Pluto Square Saturn
Natal Pluto 4th House

worth remembering that the planets are all gods and powerful archetypal energies in their own right, and can be contacted and brought into deeper relationship within. Becoming whole, integrated and spiritual involves the dissolving of inner separating barriers, which transforms this unconscious world into one of light and consciousness; and is a redemptive process of inner healing and cleansing for the individual and the world.

The God Pluto is the Lord of the Underworld, the otherworld, the dark unconscious, taking a position at the edge of the total potential of human consciousness. This is reflected and symbolised by Pluto's planetary position in the solar system, being the furthest away from the Sun and Earth in outer physical space, and correspondingly at the deepest point within inner mind space. The hermetic axiom indicates the relationship between things 'As above, so below', and 'as within, so without'. This is a core experience for those undergoing a real initiation as the previously assumed programme of physical reality dissolves and is superseded by a direct knowing that the universe is a construction of Mind creatively and imaginatively expressing itself.

The personal unconscious includes experiences of the personal existence, childhood experiences, memories, a storehouse of old thoughts, emotions, perceptions, patterns of outgrown behaviour, compulsions, obsessions, dreams, repressions. All of these still have an effect upon our conscious lives, often holding a key to problem areas, and through working with them in therapy we can often resolve such problems by integrating aspects of the unconscious into the conscious mind. Within the collective unconscious, there are elements of racial and social programming, as well as basic themes common to all humanity. These include mythological associations, images and symbols which emerge into collective consciousness and society throughout the ages, serving as a focus for group motivation and direction. Strangely, these do not seem to derive from historical traditions and tribal migrations, yet appear to be inherent in the total psyche and mind, arising almost spontaneously or as the society has an inner need for some unifying or directive symbolic image to centre upon for group solidarity. This is the realm of the archetypes, those 'building blocks' of the human psyche, the worlds of the gods, planets, mythological creatures like the Phoenix and Unicorn, the signs of the Zodiac.

When serious self-exploration commences, the seeker initially explores his own personal conscious and unconscious mind.

Today, there are many ways available in order to deepen this self enquiry, such as visualisations, pathworkings, inner journeys, dream evaluation, astrology, meditation, etc. But there is an important point to be realised: namely that it is quite possible to continue this exploration beyond the purely personal unconscious into the collective unconscious; now this can be beneficial and healing, yet the seeker needs to be aware of when the boundary line between the personal and the collective has been reached or crossed. The unconscious group mind of the collective humanity includes all potential expressions of humanity, and he can spend a lifetime exploring that sphere and just disturb his own individuality, losing a sense of centredness. What is necessary is to break out of this perpetual inner examination to become reborn upon a more inclusive 'higher level', where consciousness has been expanded and his own personal pattern of potentiality is reasserted. It is much safer working with the collective unconscious when this higher integration has already been achieved, and the essential nature of reality is understood through experience.

It appears that the point of evolution in time and space is the slow, progressive arising of consciousness from the depths of unconsciousness. The biblical fiat in Genesis, 'Let there be Light' is an indication of this, and we are contributing participants in a drama devoted to universal awakening. Our own lives reflect this innate tendency for self-consciousness to emerge, as it does over the years of childhood from the potential of the unconscious, and on a daily basis as we awake from sleep. There is a two-way flowing relationship between the spheres of mind, where the conscious contents of the heavily filtered mind dissolve continually back into the unconscious, while from the unconscious emanate our essential personality patterns and directive influential ideas and thoughts.

The unintegrated conscious mind, which is still 'separate' from its unconscious twin, has a tendency towards analysis and limitation; whereas the unconscious tends to promote a joining together, a synthesis and an expansion into a greater life. The unconscious is biased towards more non-social conditioning, but as the conscious mind looks to social grouping and conformity, there is the likelihood of inner conflict developing. The correct balance to achieve is that of integrating the twins together, where they both consciously interpenetrate each other. Working with the unconscious stimulates transformation, and the act of inner exploration and probing the unconscious mind will begin to alter the observer.

Archetypal patterns appear to be a creative wellspring for many of mankind's socialising expressions, and often appear as the prime foundations for social belief structures and conditioning ideas, albeit perhaps only partially and selectively applied. They demonstrate the apparent underlying duality of the manifested world, with archetypes of the divine Man and Woman, of Good and Evil, Light and Dark in an inner state of coexistence and interrelationship, similar to the Eastern symbols of the Tao, and Yin and Yang. In this world within, a magical dimension, we can find the planetary gods of astrology, the gods of ancient cultures and civilisations, powerful elementals of nature, inner guides, lands of myths and legends. A fertile, mysterious, shape-shifting world of the changeling, source of evocative fantasies and life-enriching vitality. It can also be a realm of demons too, of shadows, danger lurking around inner corners of the mind, where many have been sadly lost throughout history, falling prey to their own self-created phantasms. It is a level where fixed definitions are difficult to make, and it is a flexible, malleable land where things merge, breaking down the barriers of contradictions and opposites.

Within the collective mind of humanity, it appears that the archetypes act as individual and social 'building blocks', which provided a means of beginning to relate to outer reality for early man, and which are the basis of both inner and social foundation. These then develop over time into historically recognisable cultures and civilisations, and history offers a means to view long-gone cultures through the medium of their heritage of symbols and images, which offer an approach to the content of their group mind. Even today, there is still a common bond between old civilisations and our own due to the fact that these former civilisations represent earlier workings of archetypal expressions that we acknowledge as informing our own culture. These are apparently universal in nature, time-spanning, and shared by all humanity through the medium of the collective unconscious mind. They are living psychic forces operating through the medium of the common mind of humanity, and are extremely powerful, and do in fact determine the destiny of man. Many of these archetypal images and symbols have been adapted in a multiplicity of variations by mankind, and then reabsorbed through the socialising process via science, philosophy, education, religion and morality.

Where these archetypes originally come from, nobody knows.

They are like 'mind-genes', part of our genetic consciousness heritage, parallel to the physical genes inherited from our parents, being preformed psychological patterns residing within the unconscious mind. There is a saying that Nature abhors a vacuum; perhaps, then, these archetypes arose in response to an empty mind.

The Inner Shadow

Some say that an empty mind is the devil's playground, but that is just bad propaganda! Meditation is designed to decondition the seeker, to empty out the contents of the mind and thus break the spell of limiting and imprisoning social conditioning and illusion. What invariably occurs when self-work begins to make some progress, is the inner stimulation and agitation of what has been termed the 'Shadow', or in occult groups, the 'Dweller on the Threshold'.

Pluto's kingdom of Hades is an area of purgatory, of purgation, and so the Pluto energy is closely associated with this cleansing and healing activity during life too. The planet Saturn is also related to the Shadow and the Dweller, but I feel that Saturn as a teacher is more of a way-shower, a pointer to the transpersonal way. Saturn is more closely related to leading an aspirant to the threshold of the first abyss, whereas Pluto is the accompanying guide across the abyss of death of the separate individual and the subsequent rebirth on the transpersonal path. Saturn indicates a ring-pass-not of the solely personal separate life, teaching and leading to the point of transformative crisis when Pluto emerges and asserts his greater power. Pluto is also a symbol for the collective Shadow/Dweller which requires redemption, and reflecting its position in the solar system, offers a transpersonal vision for humanity to achieve before we, as 'responsible new gods', can cross beyond the threshold to take our conscious place in the greater universe that would then open up for us.

As Pluto deals with unspoken passions, taboo areas, emotional intensity, creative wildness, power and dominance in its lower human expression, then a look into the nature of the personal and collective shadow is needed. To integrate the hidden inner 'devil', to accept and to acknowledge that dark side of one's nature, is an act of self-healing, and vital for the continuity of our species. Individually, we are required to deal first with our own darkness –

and that can be hard and challenging enough for many – and then, once successful, perhaps we can join with others to work at cleansing the collective shadow. The first step is to accept and acknowledge our own repressed self; the interpretations of Pluto aspects and transits can offer some indications of where certain compulsive patterns are, and how they are expressing themselves in your life. Whilst these do not reveal the totality of an individual shadow, they do reveal certain prime aspects of it operating at a deep motivating and influential level within the psyche.

The Shadow is generally perceived as a negative entity, one to be wary of and to avoid if possible, and this attitude amplifies the reluctance of people to explore their inner nature; most have a feeling (often socially conditioned through Christianity) that lurking within is a demon looking for the way out. Our outwardly polarised society gives little credence to the necessity of inner knowledge, tending to mock, penalise and alienate those who openly promote enquiry. Essentially society is not convinced that the process of 'socialising and civilising' has gone deep enough to guarantee effective programming of its citizens. The fact is that the Shadow reflects the dualism of nature and the world of appearances, and is not all black and negative.

It is an archetypal principle, and so displays dual characteristics of good/evil, light/dark, chaos/order, etc. The Shadow embodies both unredeemed and unexpressed aspects. Apart from the healing effects of redeeming 'negative aspects', there are often positive unexpressed aspects of the individual that require release, and would contribute to a more fulfilling life.

For the majority of people, their personal centre of consciousness is termed 'I', the separate identifying ego linked to name, form and memory. It is around this created centre that we direct our lives as a result of choice and decision within our conscious mind. In fact it is a false centre, one of social convenience, an illusory creation that enforces the sense of separateness, independent islands of consciousness in the world; yet up to a certain point in unfoldment, it is a most necessary centre.

Everyone becomes aware of the fact that there are conflicting tendencies within themselves, in their emotions, mind and body. People are quite paradoxical in nature, and are often unable to achieve a state of inner reconciliation. One of the problems of modern society is the fact that social education largely ignores inner experience – and, in particular, inner conflict. As a result, as individuals mature, they have no means of coming to terms with such conflict, and it is only intensified by their solitary, unguided struggles.

What tends to occur is that those aspects which do not easily fit into those acceptable image patterns of self and society become repressed and eventually suppressed, relegated to the unconscious mind through an act of willed denial. Yet they do not cease to exist, even if the surface conflict seems to have receded. Such inner struggle reinforces the apparent strength and dominance of the egoistic 'I', which increasingly appears to assume the role of arbiter, decision-maker and judge of what it chooses to 'associate with as part of its self-image'; this image is of course determined primarily by social conditioning, and so a vicious circle is perpetuated over time and generations of social suppression.

This leads to splits occurring in the inner psyche, created by the demands of socialisation. Whilst this is understandable, what the modern world has lost and denied again is the way to heal these inner divisions – and Pluto, working through the Shadow is looking for ways to bring about a resolution and rebirth.

There are at least three major divisions enforced: the conscious 'I'; the persona-social mask; and the hidden shadow in the unconscious. The existence of multiple inner selves is revealed by those inner dialogues of conflict, of opposition between head and heart, of moral dilemmas, of life directions, problems of choice.

The inner Shadow often is not consciously seen by its carrier; it seems to evade conscious recognition, hiding 'in the corner of the eye' where any movement directed to focus upon it causes its disappearance, whilst leaving behind a residue of its existence as an intangible point of disturbance. It cannot be grasped, even though it becomes virtually a distinct self within everyone, yet often displays itself through dreams or guided meditations, symbols and imagery. Its dark face has a tendency to contaminate lives and relationships, where those elements of suppressed denial erupt at times of crisis and the personality structure begins to fragment and crumble as its assumed centre finds it difficult to cope. Yet these are times of great opportunity for self-healing! It is an image of 'the Black Man', a figure of fear and a symbol that underlies much of the world's racialist attitudes, the 'Unknown Other' who is always a danger.

One way of attempting to see where the Shadow is influencing your life is throught the phenomenon of 'projection'. This is where aspects of your denied self are projected out from your unconscious onto people or things in the outer world, without you consciously realising the fact. You then relate to these mirrored reflections which overlay your perception and experience of these people in the world, failing to understand that your perception is distorted by your own projection of denied self-aspects, and that you fail to see or relate to the real other person. These overlaid projections also tend to contain an emotionally charged content for you, where strong emotions are evoked for you, so that you cannot be neutral in respect of the person who is acting as a recipient for your Shadow projection; your emotions are extreme and polarised, and are often quite negative towards the recipient, especially when it involves tendencies that you deny as not being part of a self-image. If they are unexpressed qualities, your projection may see someone in an admiring way who appears to embody all that you wish you were yourself. The Shadow projection can also be intertwined with those of the Anima and Animus, to confuse the issue (more of them later).

It appears that the Shadow projection is overlaid upon someone of the same sex, partly because it is a part of your own personal psyche that is being extruded for understanding. Antagonisms with other men or women are a likely source to examine honestly; or those characters in a group situation that act as a repository for a group shadow to express itself upon, those who are alienated, or a butt for jokes, etc. It can be that in personal encounters, projections can be recognised when assumptions or claims about another are strongly denied and resisted by the recipient of our psychic denials (although these may also be an attempt by the other at self-denial too, and should be carefully evaluated as dispassionately and honestly as possible later, to try and determine the degree of projection).

Whilst the Shadow can be projected out into the world, upon people or races that you have no personal experience of, it is more likely to be found in the immediate environment, especially in the close intimacy of the home and family. This can cause family friction, leading at one extreme to the traditional 'black sheep' of the family, the one who does not fit in properly, whom people criticise and dislike. The impact of the Shadow tends to influence a person's behaviour in an unconscious manner, almost forcing him to act in a way that fulfils others' expectations. When one becomes excessively concerned with the actions of others, and emotionally charged (or emotionally unstable) when in direct contact with them, then there may be a psychic projection at work in the relationship. Families are based upon this sense of psychic involvement, and so this sphere of examination is difficult to apply objectively, but these elements should be considered.

The Shadow is a blind spot in individual self-assessment, covering a variety of illusions, self-images, beliefs in being 'right', and a self-righteousness that hinders creative co-operation and right relationships. For many, it becomes a sense of guilt, especially those heavily affected by guilt-enforcing religions, a sense of inner oppression from negative social programming. Often, it reveals itself in underlying tones through relationships, where what is openly said is registered by a recipient as lacking sincerity as the words contradict what is 'felt' at the time of utterance; certain politicians create this response in people, although as charismatic figures they create a response which polarises into two diametrically opposed groups registering opposing reactions.

The other face of the Shadow is that of an opponent to the false ego centre and restrictive social conditioning, and in this role it seeks to promote a true development of the unique inner potentiality (as indicated by the natal chart) where the individual breaks free of social impositions, being able to live as a truly conscious independent contributor to social advancement and healing. Such a person is not, however, bound to the innate social pattern, and whilst usually respecting the laws of the state, sees his real responsibility as being true to his own self and to allow his own destined pattern to unfold freely.

The way to allow this Shadow side to emerge is through first accepting those aspects of the self which have been denied, and then integrating them into the conscious self. This releases a harmonising and balancing energy into the psyche, and helps develop greater tolerance and understanding in social relationships. Those latent qualities and talents can then find access into your life, and expression in the outer world, finally freed from those blockages of denial.

Until individuals release the light hidden within their inner Shadow, then the world collective shadow remains a dangerous 'demon' looking for ways to escape through crisis and pain. World service starts with ourselves, and transforming ourselves and our own personal sphere of influence is the most radical revolutionary act possible. It must be remembered that a society which promotes individual external identification with social ideologies (politics, religion, nationalism) which claim and assume social acceptance is a society that will deny individual freedom, creating areas of life that will be relegated to the unconscious as they are not ideologically acceptable. This is a society that creates self-deception and illusion. Group consciousness and conformity can be either very negative or very positive. If in one instance, the self is 'misplaced' into ideological conformity through a process of penalisation and exclusion, then it is negative; if it promotes individuality and freedom whilst a unanimity of group purpose is worked towards for the benefit of all, then it is positive, and the Shadow does not develop to any excessive degree.

In the natal chart, Shadow projections can be noted, and their expression is often found in the natal sign and house where Saturn is placed. The point where the collective Shadow may be observed working through the individual's life and chart is the sign and house of Pluto. It should not be forgotten that many of the qualities and characteristics of Pluto are those which are repressed by people, or which become obsessive to varying degrees, and thus can contribute towards amplifying the power of the Shadow. Pluto's affinity with 'taboo' subjects and activity is one such source for inner denial or unease at its exposure. Attractions to varying forms of sexual expression can lead to guilt or feelings of self-disgust in certain types of personality, especially those which have previously been strongly conditioned by religious or moral teachings, or are afraid of parental or peer disapproval and rejection. Certainly Pluto has associations with all those aspects of human life that can rise to the surface, many of which are socially condemned (perhaps rightly so in some cases) and yet still exist as unresolved tendencies which haunt people. Social denial of their existence only tends to aggravate such tendencies; more social acknowledgement of the existence of taboo attractions as existing within the human complexity and a willingness to help people learn how to resolve their problems can be a redemptive road to take, providing it is achieved without undue social condemnation and stigma.

Group Participation

Pluto is the ruler of the masses, the collective group, and this is an associative identification that all members of society are encouraged to make during their formative years of growing to adulthood and to perpetuate during their adult life.

The collective group acts as a defined container – like a womb – which imposes a certain collective lifestyle, influencing the way in which the individual is allowed to perceive himself and the world. It creates a mental paradigm, a world view which is essentially immune to questioning so long as enough people maintain its supportive assumptions.

In exchange for a sense of security, of belonging and mutual support, and a socially acceptable philosophy of life, the individual relinquishes spontaneous freedom of thought and action, acquiescing in the moulding process of the particular society into which he has been born. Because of the effectiveness of this conditioning, group socialisation is extremely resistant to change, and the factor of social inertia is usually a barrier preventing forces of transformation from succeeding, unless through perseverance over time they succeed in eroding the foundations.

Whilst the fact of social manipulation by small but powerful élitist groups is acknowledged, the majority of people are still extremely resistant to any acceptance of the fact that they are mainly 'asleep', living a programmed life of automatic social responses and thought with relatively little true independence. The first step towards becoming free is to realise this. Unfortunately, the world provides considerable evidence that under the influence of varying types of mind manipulation, most still lie under the spell of the group.

Groups are formed from family, race/tribe and nation, and the unitive relationship which maintains these connections is the communality of people joining together under a need to build a group lifestyle which is of benefit to all participants. This can be a fine achievement, but often the Pluto influence upon such a grouping leads to a tendency – especially in the leaders – towards an insistence that life be lived strictly to the world view of the group or its leaders, with any deviation from this being severely penalised. This creates a society that is ruled by the power of threat and penalty, and which through its attitudes is liable to become antagonistic towards any other society that has a different world view and philosophy; hence international conflict.

Generally, societies rot from the top downwards, corruption sets in at the leadership levels where the heady effects of power and influence soon distort the perceptions and attitudes of the leaders. For the common person it is sufficient to succeed in surviving and taking care of the immediate family. It is noticeable that the Pluto influence, with its traditionally more negative characteristics, becomes increasingly prominent in leaders as their power or time in office extends. Whilst this may be more obvious in those who have a strong Scorpio/Pluto bias in their natal charts, the fact that Pluto rules the masses means that these leaders of the collective group become a conduit by which the Pluto energies enter that society.

The individual becomes dependent upon the group for his sense of identity, needing to be recognised and accepted by the group, and basically becoming subservient to it. The individual assumes an image that is socially acceptable, which is fine for the stability of society, but could be negative for personal growth and development, or creating an enlarged Shadow-self due to an inability to express socially unacceptable aspects of the personality. A new, conscious relationship is needed between the society and the individual, one which promotes and benefits both, rather than an unnatural, imposed, non-thinking relationship as is the present case. Those exploring their own natures and breaking free of their conditioning patterns are awakening into enhanced maturity, and discovering that in their own freedom and sensitive consciousness they also find a much more positive way of participating in society, based on a new relationship with the outer environment.

When those collective attitudes dominate, there is always a strong aspect of separativeness present, to help preserve the inviolability of the group view. Solidarity is evaluated in numbers, and the attitude that 'many is right' is a fixed assumption, and reverted to when there is a challenge to security. People tend to prefer to be followers, to be submissive to those who offer themselves as leaders, because this is easier than seeking a personal inner way. But the spiritual way is to use the crutch only when one cannot walk unaided, and to realise that it is foolish to keep using it when there is no need; responsibility and power should be assumed by the individual, and not handed over to a leader.

The relationship of individual to group that Pluto works with is more amplified in the examples of Pluto operating in the natal chart and through transits. In the development of societies and leaders, the Pluto effect is seen in its support for the rise of 'new movements' and the corresponding rise in countergroupings designed to change the direction of society. Opposition to the policies of new movements is inevitable, and can act as a balance and 'home for dissidents'. Pluto tends to be both builder and destroyer at once, just as at the point of birth, the seed of death becomes activated.

New forms of grouping which are based on individual awakening are considered in Chapters 7 and 8, as these provide one form of countergroups emerging in the world which embody a building energy of Pluto.

The Hidden Inner Opposites, Anima and Animus

The sphere of life most favoured by Pluto for stimulating inner transformation is that of those emotions which are experienced as a form of relationship with the outer world. Emotional responses and reactions are of prime importance in the inner experience, and through the medium of the physical senses tend to condition later intellectual evaluations of experience. Hiding within most philosophies and intellectual analyses emerging from the traditionally masculine mind are those emotional foundations and sensitivities which are traditionally the province of feminine perception.

For any idea, ideology or religion to take root in a society, there has to be a strong emotional dimension which reflects a certain 'content' (or attitude) that is found to be agreeably resonant by enough members of that society. Personal philosophies and ideals are always rooted in the emotions, irrespective of how they may be expressed in intellectual terms. That is why we take great offence when we are challenged by others who have different attitudes and beliefs to ourselves, because we are being attacked on underlyingly emotional grounds and we react emotionally. Such challenges become personal and antagonistic, and conflicts occur which even if couched in the language of the mind are essentially emotional in nature.

Our conscious sense of self develops over many years, and is an inwardly 'collective self', a grouping of often disparate conflicting elements constellated through reflections of our parents, personal experiences, and social conditioning. On the level of the separate individual self, there cannot be unity within a multiple personality; the level of reconciliation has to be achieved on a different level of our being.

Human life is a life of social relationship in a dualistic world; most human efforts are devoted to resolving the difficulties of living with each other in social groupings and in the interactions between all of the multiplicity of personal relationships that each of us have. This is a key to understanding the purpose and function of the Pluto energies, and its 'objective manifestation' during this century and the corresponding emergence of the global world state of interdependence. Pluto seeks transformation and change through the intensity and pressure of relationships, and attempts to open a channel between 'the outer and inner worlds'.

Within the unconscious mind, there is also what Jung has termed the *anima* and *animus*, which are influential archetypal images and energies which are the sexual opposite to our physical bodies; for the man, it is an inner feminine, for the woman it is an inner masculine, designed to aid an inner journey towards integration.

The essential relationship and urge to unite between the male and female sexes is affected powerfully by the inner activity of the anima and animus. This involves the attractive potency between the two opposites of energy which strive to enter into a relationship of unity, if only temporarily, and which may be perceived as the innate sexual instinct of perpetuating the species and creating new life from out of existing life. As many of us have discovered, the human experience of this impulse, and our complex emotions within relationship, can often be quite difficult, even traumatic. In many ways, our response to these urges and inner compulsions is a major factor in the way that our life develops, and our choices in partnerships are crucial in determining our enjoyment of life. Certainly Western society lacks any real training in social relating and sexual relationships, which is very regrettable, creating many social problems and anguish for people who lack psychological understanding of the inner processes at work. All of us can observe the effects of Pluto ripping through marriages and ill-formed social alliances.

The concept of anima–animus provides us with an approach to discovering why we are attracted towards certain types of partners as an expression of our own personal psychology beyond the natural mating instincts. Some seem always attracted towards what outsiders consider to be the wrong sort of partner for them, and yet an irresistible compulsion appears to lead them towards these unsatisfactory relationships, where the results are traumatic and full of suffering for all concerned. Certainly there can be several contributory reasons, but equally certain is the fact that a lack of self-knowledge is often a major factor.

Over the last twenty years, there has arisen in Western society a new interest in exploring these hidden inner opposites. The women's movement has evoked the inner masculine component of the female mind into consciousness, and, with varying degrees of success, women have integrated more 'masculine' tendencies into their inner lives and outer expression. Men have been more willing to explore their inner sensitivity and emotional dimensions which have often been repressed, and to allow space in their lives to integrate the inner feminine. These changes tend to occur within those groupings of people which are responsive to movements within the collective unconscious, and again we can note an example of the Pluto stimulation of this level of being. People are changing, people are moving towards personal integration, and the seeding in society of future trends is progressing, preparing the way for major social change. As always, such progressive seed groups are often only rewarded for their efforts by social abuse, ostracism and lack of understanding, partly created by their own lack of understanding and misinterpretation of what is occurring and by extreme responses to the inner stimulus.

The archetypal anima and animus appear to exist at an interface between the personal and collective unconscious within the psyche. They seem to be an essential seed for the qualities and characteristics which we associate with masculinity and femininity, and with those basic symbolic images which are associated with male and female. The anima archetype for the man involves his patterns of roles associated with the female, images as mother, sister, wife, witch, temptress, virgin, prostitute, confidante, womb, cup or chalice, and goddess. For the woman, the animus images can be father, brother, husband, wise man, king, warrior, spear/sword, protector and god.

Often, the human being appears as an actor in a drama forged and directed by archetypal images and symbols. Between those images arising from the inner world and those symbolised by the zodiac signs, there appears to be the fullest possible range of aspects of the personality that can be expressed in this world. Generally, each of us can only be a host to a fraction of these images, and only for short periods of time, and the scope of the personality is like a stage upon which these 'seed-gods' appear from time to time. Certain people, especially those who emerge into more public attention through media fame or charismatic qualities, are those who in some way embody a bridge to the archetypal images and world, and these people become identified in the public mind as transmitters of certain images; often, they also fall prey to the pressure and conflict of 'having' to reflect these inner associations. Politics, religion, and the entertainment media are three distinct areas which display this tendency. Actors and actresses become typecast, some gain lasting fame as embodying popular images, like Marilyn Monroe. Politicians like John Kennedy and Margaret Thatcher are almost archetypal characters, where the public perception of image around them is so potent that the reality is almost missed, and a spell-like quality persists, so that even if they assert that what is false is true, the degree of their authority and conviction persuades people that it is the truth.

For most people, the magical quality of enchantment that is created by the penetration of the world of archetypes into everyday reality is a most potent bewitchment. We often experience this through the phenomenon called 'falling in love', that age-old common experience that transforms our personal world , if only for a short time. In many ways we fall in love with a projection of the self, a mirroring of our hidden inner opposite ideal image which has been overlayed upon another who is in some way an appropriate 'hook' on which the projection can be hung. Often, the best way to become aware of the outer projection of the inner world into our social lives, is through the reflections that come back to us from others, especially those who are serving as screens for these archetypal images and aspects of self. We see this occurring in the Shadow, and in this anima–animus duality.

In a world of illusions, love certainly adds its own share of confusion and complications; it can be a supreme disillusioner. Falling in love shakes and shatters personal foundations, rearranging them into new patterns, where emotions can run rampant, the serpent of sexuality leads us into compulsive activity and all those competing inner selves are thrown into the air creating a peculiar form of inner disintegration. Pluto watches in amused silence whilst the anima–animus projections are still vitalised; Pluto knows that his time will come later.

The projection onto the other of the ideal man or woman tends to occur at the onset of the love relationship. To a greater or lesser degree, any intimate love relationship involves such projection. In all relationships with the opposite sex, there is an element of projection at work which often remains unrecognised. For those intent on self-exploration, reintegrating the Shadow and their inner opposite is quite vital balancing work, in a personal and social context.

One sign that the projection is occurring is the obsessive quality of fascination and preoccupation related to the other, linked with those potent emotions of attraction–repulsion–desire. Sometimes, this can become a one-sided unrequited love, which can be very difficult to handle, because somehow the projection has to become reclaimed and reabsorbed into the projecting self; otherwise it can feel that you have lost an essential part of your being, and the awareness of incompleteness and disintegration is undeniable; yet how to heal the inner divisions is the problem. It must be remembered that especially in today's society, when there is a lack of a tradition related to the inner world, and common socially created bridges to link with it, that the only way it can find to communicate with people is through this means of projection outwards. The real purpose is to bring about a metamorphosis, a turning within where the potential of harmony and integration can be discovered.

Often, the projection is mutual, with anima evoking a corresponding awakening within the animus, and a partnership becomes a four-sided relationship, inner and outer. Such attractions have an irresistible quality, as though the whole universe is conspiring to bring about an intense relationship for its own mysterious purposes, and an atmosphere of destiny and fate seems to swirl around the participants. Some call this karma, and consider it a recommencement of relationships from past lives; others shrug their shoulders, unconcerned about such 'explanations', but still register the sense of weirdness about it all.

Under the domination of these inner images, each falls in love with his or her own ideal partner, who is believed to be the particular person onto whom the projection has been fastened, and whom in their own perception they have just recreated as the 'perfect' man or woman. The power of love is in its transformatory effect in dissolving barriers between people, to take people out from private, isolated and separatist worlds into social relationship, mutual support, sharing and caring, and to expand the quality, content and depth of life. The difficulties start when the glamour begins to wane, and real life and real people begin to appear again.

Swept by powerful emotions, living in a 'new world' of wanting someone, and being wanted in love, with the resultant amplification of moods – it can be a dangerous crash when the balloon bursts. All of the inner qualities of each person and their characteristics are stimulated under the impact of archetypal projections, be they negative or positive; and when the honeymoon is over each is left with challenges in the relationship and previously projected parts of the self which need reintegration. It is a difficult transformation to achieve in relative harmony, especially if a formal marriage has been made, or children have been born or are on the way.

Expectations, and disappointment as the real face of the other appears, can eventually lead to the disintegration of the relationship, as the realisation dawns that the other is not living up to the ideal image. Attempts to manipulate and change the other are made, often with little success, or with resulting resentment, and friction replaces the early bliss. But this phase, during which many relationships founder, is fertile ground for transformation. As the projections become reabsorbed, the time is ripe for a reappraisal of self and other, and of the relationship, in the light of the changes wrought in the fires of love. The potential then exists for a progressive unfoldment of a higher integration within the partnership and the individual participants, that of the *coniunctio*, the mysterious union of opposites, of physical and psychic elements, as attempted by alchemists.

The personal anima–animus is a combination of elements from various sources, and an attempt at self-exploration requires an untangling of its webs in order to see and understand these elements at play in the personal life. Part derives from hereditary instincts and the sexual urge to mate and procreate; part from personal experience of the opposite sex from the time of birth, especially of the mother and father; part from the collective social tradition and relationship between the sexes; and part from the hidden personal inner opposite. Always the projection will be of a 'superpartner', one who is essentially larger than life and a fantasy or fiction. Frustrated expectations can kill any relationship, and, as in the rest of life, the sooner illusions can be punctured the better.

Amongst other characteristics, the anima-driven man tends to look for a sense of heightened feeling, emotion and relatedness with the other, which breaks down those imposed barriers of masculinity, rationalism, impersonality and lack of intimate contact (excluding purely physical sexuality). A desire to be wanted and to belong, to be nurtured within a secure womb-like home, to be cared for, is often noticeable, as the harshness and hard quality of being male is softened by the outer and inner feminine. For the animus woman, an attraction towards the more mental aspects is often noticeable, towards the impersonal, rational and logical spirit of analysis and thought; or towards the physicality of men without any emotional complexity or disruption to cause confusion within the feelings which she lives with as part of being feminine. The wise man, the good father and provider, the hard warrior – are some of the directions for the animus to strive towards.

For those pursuing inner journeys, explorations of the underworld via guided imagery, ritual or meditations, whenever you come across those inner figures of guides there lurks the presence of the anima–animus. Be co-operative, and open to entering into the inner relationship with them.

Pluto, God of the Underworld always re-enters relationships as the projections are being reabsorbed, and never again leaves, as there is always scope for possible change to occur, especially if things begin to stagnate, or personal domination occurs. Some analysis and attempt at understanding the inner unconscious world is essential to have a context within which to see how Pluto is operating through the various factors in the natal chart; he is present beneath the surface and stimulating the archetypal energies to become active in the individual and society. To Pluto, stagnation is anathema; perpetual change is the potential of 'life more abundantly'.

CHAPTER 4

Pluto and Planetary Aspects

THE NATAL ASPECTS OF PLUTO need to be carefully analysed, as they hold essential information concerning the more obvious ways that Pluto will operate and reveal its activity through the natal chart. They become intrinsic patterns of personality expression, and because of their peculiar compulsive and obsessive nature should generally be quite recognisable even if not personally acknowledged or accepted. It can be an interesting exercise to study your own major Pluto aspects, and see how strongly you are conditioned by their influence.

A basic overview of the nature of the five major aspects may be useful at this point.

THE MAJOR ASPECTS

Conjunction

The conjunction, or close proximity of at least two planets, is usually considered to be the most potent aspect. This involves a merging of the undiluted energies and characteristics of the planets which are in conjunction, and can be seen as a channel through which the functions of these planets can be more easily expressed via the personality. Often, these combined tendencies are asserted with considerable vigour by the individual, who may consciously recognise that they are expressions of personal power and individuality in social situations, yet this assertiveness is often achieved with a less than conscious awareness of its impact upon others.

There is an ambiguity about the influence of the conjunction, often derived from the nature of this inner tension and the challenge of blending energies which may well be uncomplementary or even antagonistic in nature. This often reveals itself in life as creating certain difficulties in relationships with others, especially in those situations where you may need to moderate or control your initial forms of response in order to prevent friction occurring. Such a 'life skill' may need to be learnt for social living, but it should never be over-used so that you develop a pattern of inhibition of your thoughts and feelings when in company; it is a form of sensitivity to the fact that in certain situations it may be wiser and more harmonious to remain quiet. Certainly this blended energy almost insists on its need to be expressed, and channels for this are consciously looked for in the relevant spheres of life.

Much depends upon the relative affinity of the planets in conjunction as to the ease and efficacy with which a person can apply these energies in daily life. They can flow almost 'magically' together, enabling certain talents and qualities to emerge spontaneously and miraculously into effective creative channels once a focused attempt at drawing them through has been made. The right use of the personal resources is then achieved for the benefit of the individual and ideally for others too. If the planets are lacking affinity or ease of collaboration, then utilising the energy will be more difficult, and an inner struggle is likely to create inner adjustments to enable the energies to work better with each other. A conjunction is a point of concentrated power in the natal chart if it can be properly released through the appropriate area of life – signified by its natal house position.

Sextile Aspect (60 degree aspect)

The sextile indicates a natural energy relationship between the planets involved, and has a particular association with the mental level. According to which planets are involved, indications are given as to the nature of the person's mind and the likely natural content of the thought patterns. It facilitates the ability to absorb information, collating and connecting fragments of knowledge into a synthesising comprehension, and is an integrative function of the mind, being revealed through the person's actions and ability to communicate with others. It is often associated with a talent for creative expression, especially using words, and helps to build a catholic mental outlook on life based on the ability to grasp the intellectual knowledge and cultural developments of man. There is an openness about the influence of the sextile that aids harmony, as it is not closed-minded in its inner effect, and this is conducive to the development of curiosity, space for new/other perceptions, and an ease in the wider social environment and in group co-operation.

Trine Aspect (120 degree aspect)

The trine is a positive reconciliatory aspect, capable of uniting in a working manner two apparently opposing energies, hence its symbol being like a triangle. A trine is suitable for resolving areas of difficulty that may be experienced by other hard or challenging aspects which are made to either of the planets. As this symbol of the triangle is associated with Pluto in understanding and resolving dualism, the trine aspects involving Pluto and any other planet are likely to hold a key to processes of personal integration, healing and transformation, and should be carefully considered in this light.

Square Aspect (90 degree aspect)

The square aspect between planets indicates an energy relationship of tension and challenge, which will not be resolved without some form of internal adaptation. Potentially, the results of working with the square can lead to greater inner harmony, but this is likely to occur only after prolonged effort and psychological frustration, through which fires the character has been reborn in some essential way. It often seems to indicate barriers in the individual psyche which repeatedly block a chosen route, and is reminiscent of the challenges held by the natal house of Pluto. There are 'lessons and challenges' that the square represents that cannot be avoided, inevitable crises that will require confronting as stages along the path of life. Squares are frustrating, a source of inner conflict which unless the nettle of challenge is grasped, will have a negative effect upon the life and thwart many a desire and intention. If the square is 'overcome', then it serves as a point of release for power and energy which can be applied to achieve personal aims. The square is associated with internal psychological problem areas, and an attempt to restructure the inner life, mind or emotions is vitally necessary.

Opposition Aspect (180 degree aspect)

The opposition is often more concerned with the outer objective world and with relationships with others, but unless the personal focus is entirely orientated towards achievement in the outer world it is likely to prove less of a constant personal struggle than the square. Whereas the square is more of a private personal challenge, oppositions tend to be projected outwards (similar to the Shadow) onto others, thus creating an eventual context where they can be realised, observed and worked with as psychological projections. There can be signs of compulsive behaviour, demands made upon others, expressions of the power of focused will and self-absorption which often have an interfering effect within close life relationships, coupled with attempts to manipulate others and situations for personal gain.

Creative and harmonious relationships can help to resolve the conflict between the opposition of planetary energies. Also, any trines or sextiles which are made to either opposition planet can help to resolve the problems.

SUN–PLUTO ASPECTS

Sun–Pluto Conjunction

In order to achieve the ambitions and desires which your natal Sun sign directs you towards, you will apply the Pluto energy which acts as an amplifier of your will-power. Potentially, this conjunction can be very valuable in enabling you to reach your objectives, but to maximise your chances of eventual success, you may need to make several adjustments in your temperament and attitudes.

Pluto will confer powers of regeneration and rebirth, so you should find that you are able to transform yourself, and to some degree your immediate environment, into a form that can express your purpose. Once you can determine your direction and underlying intention, you will be able to see what requires changing as a prerequisite of achievement, and then begin to apply your will accordingly.

The energy released by this aspect will tend towards extremism, with beliefs, ideas and opinions being expressed with force and

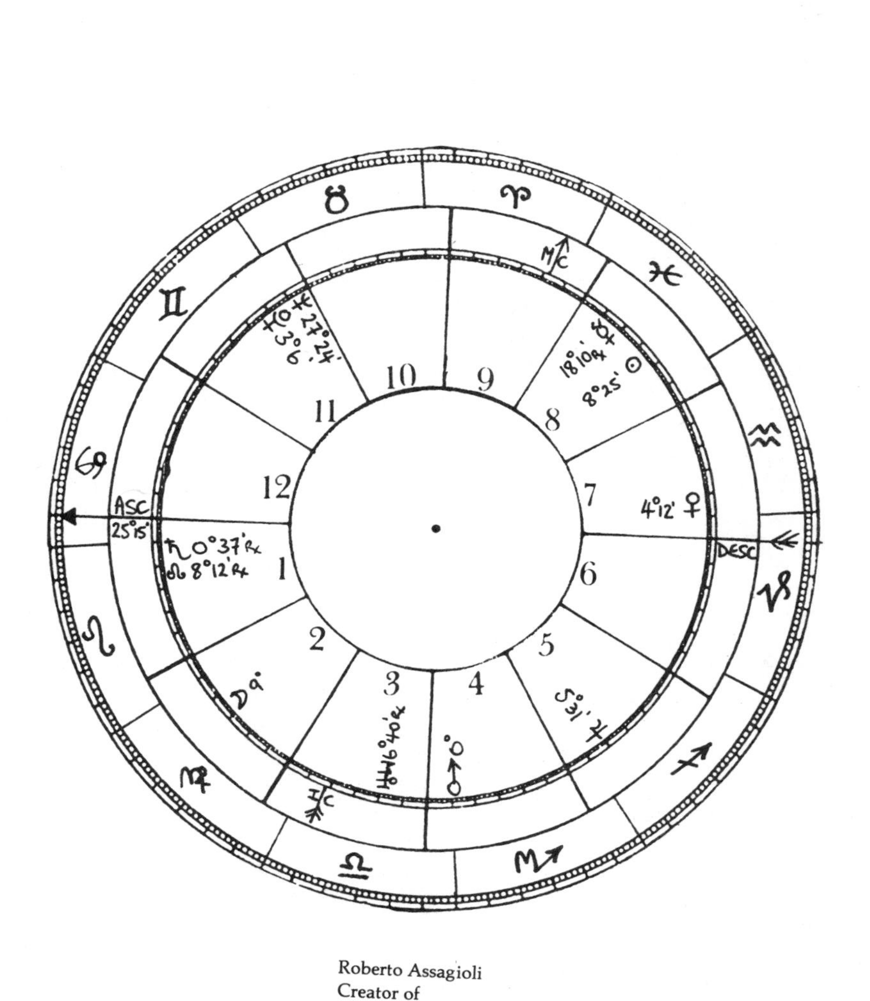

Roberto Assagioli
Creator of
Psychosynthesis
Pluto Square Sun
Square Moon
Trine Venus
Opposition
Jupiter
Sextile Saturn
Conjunct
Neptune
Natal Pluto 11th House

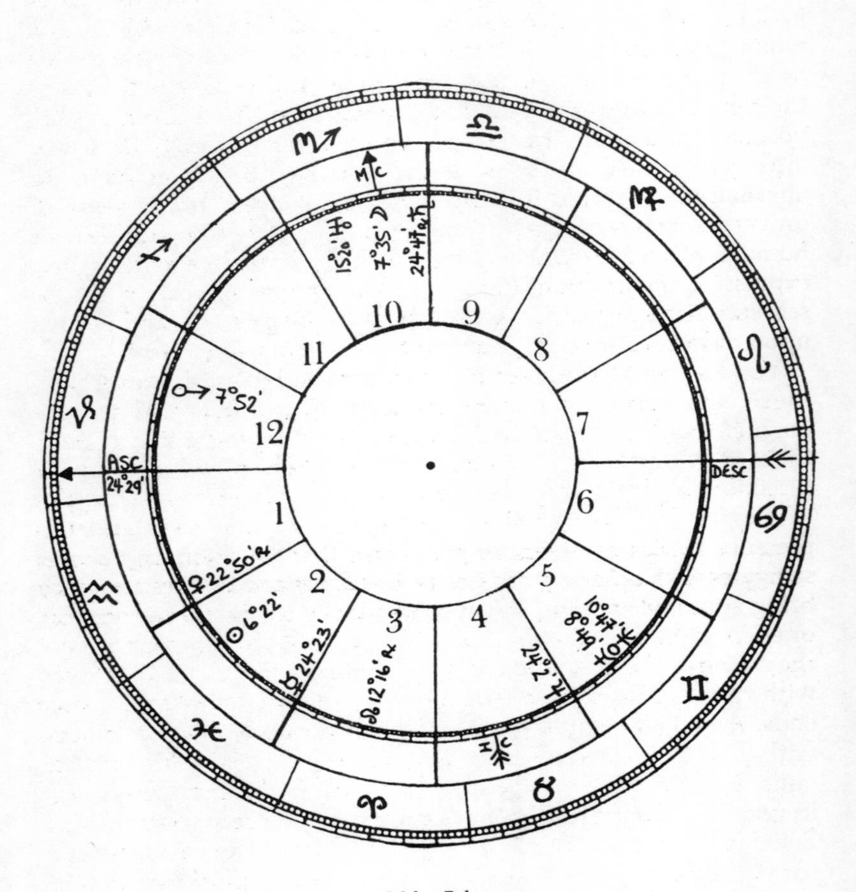

Meher Baba
Avatar, silent guru
Pluto Square Sun
Pluto Conjunct
Neptune
Natal Pluto 5th House

intensity. You will feel quite clear about your personal preferences in life, and your attitudes could be polarised into 'black and white', with no space for 'grey' to be considered, or to be accepted as a viable alternative in life. Once your choices are made, it is as though you have inscribed them on tablets of stone; even though you have the ability to change, you will not willingly do so, or alter your fixed attitudes unless you feel that you have no alternative. You find it difficult to be balanced, in the sense of universal toleration and understanding of the frailties of humanity, and probably adopt a fairly hard-line philosophy, expressing the opinion that people can change their lives and be self-sufficient if they want to, instead of being weak and relying upon others – although you tend to resist change yourself.

You will tend to be assertive, and attracted towards power, and those who appear to possess influence over others will act as a magnet to you, at least in the sense that you would like to be in their position. Such an inner desire is likely to influence your direction in life, in your work and career, or even in the struggles of family life. You will use manipulation and psychological pressure tactics as levers to guarantee that you win any power struggles with others; your one-pointedness and ruthlessness may bring apparent success, but may also bring an increasing number of enemies in their wake. You will have to learn that you are not the centre of the universe and that ultimately you cannot get away with riding roughshod over others in order to achieve your own ends. An adjustment in terms of becoming more aware of others, with their feelings, and their own unique outlook on life being as valid as yours are, would create a much more harmonious energy in your life and the fulfilment of successful personal relationships. Being willing to accept failure sometimes would be a positive step for you, to diffuse tension and to break the compulsive search for success; otherwise, you will become obsessed with achieving your goal and more willing to damage others in the interests of doing so – apart from the fact that failure will eat away at your self-esteem.

Almost paradoxically, you will also react strongly to social injustices, and may be attracted towards the alleviation of social problems. Movement in this direction is dependent upon the degree to which you become aware of the needs of others, and in so doing, reduce your own personal need for power and success. The key factor is whether you are self- or other-orientated; this will determine your responses to social humanity. Your attitude will be either 'They can change and help themselves' or 'I will change and use my power to help others to help themselves'. Such a step would involve a realignment of your self-centred self with a higher inner ideal and purpose, and would represent your becoming an integrated and responsive member of humanity.

Much of your energy will carry a sexual potency, and irrespective of your physical sex, will have a penetrative quality to it and a masculine, aggressive, thrusting nature. Your physical needs will be strong, and you will have a one-pointed directness about your desires, and will pursue your 'prey' without deviation once your choice is made. Elements of struggle and manipulation will be present in your relationships and you will take any rejection hard as it negatively affects your self-image. However, your relationships will be very intense, and you will give a wholehearted commitment to them whilst they last, becoming very emotionally involved.

In fact, your emotional understanding is likely to be a weak spot for you, at least until certain transformations have occurred within you which break down your self-preoccupation. You will experience feelings of almost dissolving into passionate relationships, losing yourself in absorption with your lover, and becoming obsessed with the affair. Such experiences could be the key to your transformation, or could fill you with fear for your personal sanity and chosen purpose so that you begin to reject such intensity for more superficial physical relationships and energy release without the emotional dimension being involved.

Sun–Pluto Sextile

With this aspect, you should be able to use the Pluto energy in a positive and constructive manner. You will be quite resourceful, and able to direct your will towards achieving your intentions, believing that with clear motivation and direction you will be able to succeed in your goals. Also, you will have considerable powers of endurance, and this will help you to persevere through tapping your inner resources.

You have several natural talents, which you can use both for your own benefit and for that of others. Communication is one talent, and you should be able to transmit your thoughts clearly to others, fluently and with style. It is likely that you will work closely with groups of people, possibly through mutual ideologies aimed towards the resolution of problems in society, as you feel a personal responsibility to work towards social betterment. You particularly dislike to see injustice done to the 'underdog', and you will not tolerate social disorder and chaos; you prefer to approach such challenges using your will and perseverance in a direct encounter, believing that your intensity will win through eventually.

You can evolve into a spokesman for such a group endeavour, as you tend to give inspiration to people who respond well to the aura of powerful energy that you emit, creating a confidence in your integrity and abilities to further the cause. For your immediate associates, the energy has a harmonising effect. You tend to use it as a personal guide to determine the right approach to take in a situation, almost as a form of psychic intuition, which takes the place of logic and analysis; you rely on this sense of directive feeling to make necessary decisions, although it can be difficult for you to express your reasons to others in a convincing way.

A natural understanding of the life process should be evident, where you have an acceptance that progression eventually requires the releasing of the old restrictive patterns, and this you are able to do as part of your own process of regeneration without much trauma. In fact, you have a capacity for ongoing creative growth in your relationships, achieved without unnecessary drama or crisis, almost as a natural evolutionary expression of the aspect's energy. You may need to review your relationships and social expression periodically, and this serves as the impulse to transform if necessary, but without undue force or pressure.

Sun–Pluto Trine

The relationship between the energies of the two planets is more naturally harmonious with this aspect. You should have the usual qualities of the ability to concentrate and to apply your will-power, coupled with the potential of regenerative transformation necessary to achieve a deeper self-integration and your chosen aims.

You will be less influenced by the undermining quality of the Pluto energy, provided that you utilise your natural gifts in socially acceptable ways. You will be able to make maximum use of whatever innate resources you possess, turning them to your advantage in achieving your goals. You will display a social awareness, and will feel attracted towards applying your talents to improving the social environment, and the fact that you seem to have a natural insight into resolving problems in the most effective manner can lead to a possible career or vocation in challenging problem-solving areas. You will have certain financial skills, and a logical and deductive mind, preferring to tackle projects where you appear as though you are reclaiming order from chaos. This gives a sense of satisfaction, as you dislike chaos and lack of distinct order; whether in your life or in your environment you want to be in control and create an ordered harmony.

You have the potential to be a spokesman or leader, where your vitality gives the impression of purposeful direction, and your mainly optimistic and fiery creative expression can attract support to you. This occurs naturally, without the usual Pluto desires for power and manipulative influencing of others; indeed, you have little compulsive desire for leadership.

You are likely to have an intuitive ability which can offer you clear insights into situations, possibly even a degree of clairvoyance, which any exploration into yoga, meditation and ways of self-discovery could release and amplify. There may be a healing energy from you, possibly aiding others who can absorb excessive energy releases by you on an unconscious level, and you can be a reliable support to a partner or anyone else who requires help in resolving problems.

You may benefit from what appears to be 'luck' in your life; this can come from inheritances, or by the ill fortune of others. You have a considerable creative potential, but to release this fully, you may have to experience some inner transformation which dissolves the blocks which are frustrating your success; this involves learning how to use this energy aspect to full advantage. Assuming that you are able to channel this energy towards socially beneficent results, and do not try to evade facing and resolving any important personal problems that arise within yourself or within a relationship, then you should experience few of the traditional difficulties implied by the Pluto energy – which for many people could be considered a blessing.

Sun–Pluto Square

The energy and challenges released by this square can be difficult to deal with, where the negative tendencies normally associated with Pluto are fully present. At best, arriving at a conscious and clear understanding of certain aspects of your nature will serve to minimise the more negative and destructive effects of this abrasive energy, and allow you to turn it into more personally positive channels. However, you would have to remain aware of how you are expressing it, as the peculiar quality of the energy would still be vitalised, and it cannot be nullified, only used in a wiser manner.

The Pluto tendencies of ambition, force, power, domination, aggression and extremism will also exist as motivating and compulsive factors in your character. You will tend to believe that your focused will-power can act in a magical way, achieving your desires and purposes by the wielding of your concentrated will; often, you will 'magically' succeed but there is usually some form of hidden price to pay. In fact, applying your potent will can often lead to more negative and destructive results that oppose your initial intention; in a sense, like the Scorpion, you are liable to sting yourself and others.

You will experience considerable inner tension as a result of this energy relationship, often finding it difficult to 'break through barriers' which appear to stand between yourself and your goals. This is Pluto attempting to force you towards an inner transformation, the need for which you will recognise whenever your inner pressure of frustrated intentions increases, until you find it hard to live with and in some way 'blow up', releasing the energy pressure. Some change will occur as a result of a powerful cathartic experience, which will enable you either to move forward towards success, or to create a new route for you to follow.

Your attitude towards authority is ambivalent. Whilst you have certain leadership qualities, and managing ability, you are often antagonistic towards those in authority, sceptical, subversive and iconoclastic in your speech and thoughts about them. Obviously, this will not lead to progress in many fields of society, but you are too independent and free-spirited to be subservient. It is likely that others will maintain a psychological distance from you, because your 'emanation' often suggests – in an unconscious manner – that you are 'dangerous'; that your way of looking at things is potentially challenging and transformative, and that a deeper involvement would bring about some unknown change in them. Others could find it a fascinating energy, and greatly enjoy your company; much depends upon the ability to handle it.

You are often looking for adversaries to pit yourself against as a personal test and for enjoyment, feeling like a fiery warrior at war. This can be expressed on all levels, physical, emotional and mental. You may not always express it in tangible terms, often entering into the adversarial state of mind within yourself, mentally enacting imaginary battles with an opponent in terms of ideological disagreement and inner dialogue; and you hate the thought of losing.

You will be hard to understand, appear quite enigmatic to many, and may often have a resistance to becoming emotionally involved with others. This is because you are aware of your emotional depths and strength of feelings, and the intensity can make you feel extremely uncomfortable, especially if you lose control when you have fallen in love. You have a fear of not being in full control, and will usually try to create a context in a relationship where you feel in command of the situation. Whilst giving an impression of great self-control and balance, you often hide the evidence of inner turmoil, which can erupt as overreactions to trivial unimportant events in your life, or be forcefully released when someone 'presses the buttons', evoking a response.

You prefer stability in your life, and are often resistant to change, especially when you have established a pattern which suits you. There can be a form of apprehension concerning actually achieving your purposes; sometimes you make good progress, only to run out of interest at the point when the final effort should be made. You should learn to acknowledge the aid of others in your life, and be open to all suggestions from others, as they can often indicate the direction in which to travel. Compromise and co-operation are two lessons which need to be learned as soon as possible, as well as more moderation in your life and expression. Once you achieve a balance between being receptive to others and your tendency to dominate, desiring them to submit to you, then you should find that the quality of your relationships begins to improve in a creative and constructive manner.

Ideally, you should redirect this abrasive energy internally. This may not be easy, and can involve some personal suffering, but it has the potential to stimulate a radical transformation to occur, which would benefit you considerably, and make life much more fulfilling for you and for those involved with you.

Sun–Pluto Opposition

With this energy working in you, most of your problems and challenges will arise in the area of interpersonal relationships, often created or stimulated by your own expression of this energy, which requires a deeper understanding and inner adjustment to be achieved before you will benefit consistently from its power.

Your temperament will be assertive, aggressive and extremist, and you will tend to use your powerful will like a sledgehammer to achieve your objectives. You prefer to force situations so that you are ready to take the advantage before anyone else can, or will act through impulse without fully considering any consequences of following your desires and aims. Your will and personality can seem to others a little overbearing, provocative and dominating, especially as you always prefer to be fully in control of all situations, and hate to feel unsure of your ground or that there is nothing you can do to influence circumstances in your favour. This is why you desire to be in a position of authority, calling the tune and writing the rules, yet are so anti-authority when roles are reversed; you then use your influence to be subversive and manipulate others to resist authority.

Socially, you will feel a desire to change the world into your image, to reflect the way that you think it should be. As virtually everyone else is attempting the same in small or large ways, inevitably you may experience conflict with others who do not agree with your panacea for the ills of the world. If you attempt to dictate to people, expressing yourself too forcefully, you may easily fail to get the right kind of support and co-operation, especially if it is made clear that you intend to be the king-pin and final arbiter. Such dominating and forceful personalities usually alienate their more creative supporters, and are left with 'mere followers' who remain with the 'leader' in sycophantic acquiescence.

Without proper awareness and understanding, these energy tendencies can become negatively expressed, eventually to your detriment; with awareness, they can become extremely positive tools to be used in socially creative ways. You will need to undergo a period of self-regeneration, to acknowledge the rights of others to assert themselves and to be themselves, not mere adjuncts to your will. More harmonious and successful relationships are possible, especially when your need for self-assertion diminishes through enhanced self-understanding and confidence in your own worth and identity. This can involve learning to rely more on yourself to achieve your own aims, rather than having to manipulate others into unconsciously aiding your private intentions. Inner changes leading to less aggressive attitudes in working with others, more co-operation to achieve mutual goals and less innate suspicion of others plus a degree of compromise in your attitudes will certainly bring more benefit to you and others.

MOON–PLUTO

Moon–Pluto Conjunction

This indicates that you will experience very strong emotions and feelings, the intensity of which can seem to dominate your choices and decisions, almost as if you are losing control over any free will. As the underlying 'triggers' acting as stimulation for your emotional experiences are often located in the unconscious mind, you may feel that there is a compulsive or obsessive fate at work in your life.

Relationships are the main sphere where you will encounter the potentially transformative impact of this energy, where you meet your destiny, and this sphere will have a major influence upon your life direction. The conjunction's energy is likely to be applied towards an emotional domination of others, influencing them and events in your favour, possibly by a tendency to exploit others' feelings for you, especially as lover or parent. There can be periodic crises, as though repressed emotional energy is rising up to the surface in you, and it demands that it is quickly released. This energy explosion can take the form of 'a volcano erupting', leading to family friction and confrontation between partners and children, even to sudden dramatic major life changes apparently arising spontaneously. For you, the necessary release is crucial, even if it demands that you suddenly let go of everything that you had previously been building and burn your bridges to the past.

You can be quite moody, reflecting the ebb and flow of the moon's tides, and you will search for depth and intensity within your intimate relationships. You have a high ideal of what you assume to be a perfect partner for you, and often would prefer to remain alone rather than become involved with others who do not fit this ideal, preferring to wait for your destined mate. In many ways, you are looking for the physical embodiment of your inner partner image, your anima or animus figure, which you project outwards onto real people to see if they can compare.

In love, you will be very committed to the relationship, loving very deeply, almost being consumed in fire by the strength and nature of your feelings. It is likely to be an obsessed state for some time, often difficult to handle, being a total preoccupation for you during the early stages of the affair. You will be very possessive and demanding of your partner, possibly too critical once you realise that they are not the ideal partner that you initially believed them to be. You will hate any rejection, especially if your emotions are still fully engaged with your ex-lover, as the passion will turn back on yourself for want of a recipient, and burn you. There can be a thin line between love and hate sometimes, and you are likely to understand something of emotional masochism and sadism.

Your relationships can often be emotionally destructive, often for all concerned, where passions are intense and people lose themselves in the emotional fires, being changed either positively or negatively in the process, but certainly emerging as different people to the ones they were when they entered the relationship. You will need to develop an ongoing evaluation of any relationship, to ensure that each is benefiting from its continuance, and that it is an uplifting energy, not one which enslaves in the name of love.

You can be a little impatient and domineering in style, and your close friends are likely to be few, only those who can accept inner intensity and depth, rather than a preoccupation with triviality, especially as you experience your emotions so strongly all the time. In a family environment, you will have to guard against using a tyrannical will on people, learning to bend and compromise more to live harmoniously with others.

If you can succeed in learning how to allow your emotional energies to rise easily to the surface, and to develop relationships and suitable channels for the energy to be poured into in a constructive way, then most of the main difficulties of this aspect will be resolved. Any repression of your emotions will create more problems, leading to the likelihood of emotional crises and explosions, and should be avoided if possible. Also, you need to develop a greater understanding of how your ideal partner has to be found in real life, and not as an unreal (in the physical world) male or female archetype within yourself. Emotional maturity, depth, intensity and understanding are potentially there to be unfolded by you, provided that you pass through the transformation of self that Pluto is seeking to bring about, as focused in your emotional nature.

Moon–Pluto Sextile

This is a more harmonious aspect with Pluto, which is likely to confer a fundamental faith in life, that all will work out well, and that you are able to apply your will to direct your imagined purpose into reality.

You should have less problems with emotional intensity and compulsive patterns of behaviour, and will feel more inwardly secure, even to being quite emotionally self-sufficient. In relationships, you may appear somewhat withdrawn into your own preoccupations at times, and this can appear as though you are a little cold and uninvolved. This is not the case, however, as love is important to you, and necessary for your emotional well-being; but you are not totally dependent upon the other for your stability and focus in life. You tend to have a more intellectual experience and understanding of love, rather than the sheer passion and intensity that is often associated with Pluto energy; the sextile appears to balance the energy more naturally and easily, although you still possess the ability to renew and transform outdated emotional and lifestyle patterns, replacing them with more suitable ways of expression.

You have an interest in observing others, trying to perceive their motivations and ways of looking at things; this can help to expand and enrich you, apart from serving to dissolve any fixed attitudes or belief patterns in you, that are perhaps limiting. You are sensitive to the feelings of others, and will develop a concern and sense of responsibility for social reform to improve the quality of life. You may enter some sort of work related to public service, perhaps more in an administrative or management role rather than in a directly caring position, as you have skills in business and organisation. Working with younger people may attract you, and you are likely to have a natural affinity with them, being concerned about their future life and place in society. You will use your energy and ability to communicate fluently in situations which require a harmonising energy, and you will always try to live and to express yourself in ways which ensure that harmony is maintained.

In directing your life, you will try to apply the principle that 'Energy follows Thought', that visualising your intention clearly is the first step towards making it real, and that thought is itself an energy that can bring about your purpose. Seeing this work in real life amplifies your essential faith that 'life is on your side', and gives you confidence to follow your own path.

Moon–Pluto Trine

This aspect will give you a sense of basic inner security, allied to a naturally self-assured confidence in your own personal strength and ability to cope successfully with challenging situations.

You will experience a depth and intensity to your emotions, which you will tend to keep under a degree of self-imposed control by your will, as you have a fear of allowing them free expression; this fear will be built upon real life experiences, where you have lost emotional control in evocative circumstances, and you are reluctant to let go fully again.

It is likely that you will have an intuitive form of insight into people, a penetrating perception of their hidden nature and motivations which still leaves you with a fundamentally caring nature. You will freely give support and aid to close friends when in need, and have a particular soft spot where children are concerned. With this tendency, you may be attracted towards working in a public or social capacity with people; or where your ability to resolve problems can find areas of social challenge, or involve aspects of financial management.

You will often apply a technique which involves creative use of your imagination and will, whereby these energies will be directed towards manifesting your thoughts into real life, thus actively creating your own life-pattern according to your personal desires. You will have a natural ability to conjoin will and imagination that many would envy, and for you it comes quite easily; make the most of this talent, but ensure that your envisioned intentions have right motivation behind them, or the results will become negative for yourself and others.

In your intimate relationships, you will expect high quality, and so you will be especially careful in choosing partners for longer-term relations or marriage. It is likely that you will want children, and that the birth of a family will have a considerable impact upon you, giving you a more mature and responsible outlook. Your feelings will be very tied to the family and home, and you will put much effort into making it work successfully for all concerned, and would be reluctant to throw it away on the temporary satisfaction of any personal desires.

Moon–Pluto Square

The energy released by this aspect can create difficulties in your personal relationships and in your inner emotional life, which will be experienced as intense and extreme. There may be an atmosphere of emotional brooding around you, which psychically can make others prefer to keep a distance from you as they register a feeling of elemental danger.

The theme of control is again crucial and dominating; you feel that you have to remain constantly in control of your own emotions and also try to control your immediate environment by the force of your presence to avoid any 'threats' from others. This leads towards dominance in your relationships as the way to control, being very demanding that others conform to your desires and wishes, but which creates imbalance in the relationship. You intend to 'rule the roost', and will never willingly take a submissive position. If forced to do so, you will undermine any assumed superiority on the part of your senior. You can react almost violently towards the efforts of anyone who tries to change you, and you may become even more extreme in your expression of that part of your nature which the other person wishes to change.

You are a natural 'loner', a little impatient, potentially aggressive in attitude unless carefully controlled and moderated, expressing yourself in a straight, direct style often lacking in social graces and diplomacy, abrasive and brusque, especially with those for whom you feel little respect. This can create problems at work and socially, but these do not particularly bother you, as you feel it more important to be as true to yourself as possible; what you do need to learn is how to do that and maintain a constructive and positive reationship with others, to gain an insight into the interdependence of people and to work within that in a harmonious manner, and not just be destructive.

You hate being restricted and chafe against any bonds that you feel are imprisoning you, even if it was you who initially bound yourself for reasons which existed at the time. You are ambivalent towards the past, and often you just want to forget it totally as having no relevance to you now, and then at other times you express a loving kind of attachment to it, attempting to invoke it again in some way. At least you know the past; the future sometimes scares you, giving a feeling of unease, especially as you cannot control it as you would like. You can find it difficult to live with those powerful feelings of destructive energy inside you, the urge to smash and break down all barriers in your life that are preventing you from experiencing 'freedom'. These build considerable tensions and inner pressures that you have to control and repress, because unleashed in the wrong way and at an inappropriate time they would cause much damage to yourself and your family. It can be hard for others to understand how this sensation of destructive emotional energy conditions much of your personal expression. It is also difficult for you to discover satisfactory ways of releasing this energy into constructive channels, but essential that you do succeed to prevent confrontations throughout your life. Often, you may tend to force issues, releasing the energy in a confrontational way to bring about sudden dramatic changes in your life, purely as a release valve to the build-up of inner pressure, which increases as you feel that you are not controlling your life, or directing it along paths which you know are right for you. The tendency is to explode, or to implode, to trigger off the necessary transformation required to create space for new life to occur.

What you need to do is to begin to trust more, to trust your family and intimate partners, to share more easily and communicate these inner difficulties so that others can help you to release them less abrasively. Compromise is essential; the world does not revolve around your needs and desires, and living together requires a mutuality of benefit and support. A redirection of your self-preoccupied energy towards aiding others could serve as a positive channel for your emotional intensity to flow out in a harmonious way, and reduce your inner pressure. A deeper understanding of human nature, perhaps through courses and study in psychology, occultism, meditation and self-exploration, would benefit you considerably, and give an insight into those energies and levels of consciousness that combine to create the complexity of the human personality.

Moon–Pluto Opposition

The energy of the opposition aspect can create emotional blockages, making it difficult for you to express your feelings and leading to a build-up of emotionally based energies which cannot find a way to be released. As with the square aspect, this gives you the tendency to maintain a tight inner control, which can influence your personal expression in relationships with an atmosphere of repressed violence and passion. At times, you can be like a coiled snake waiting for a target to come into striking distance, just so you can unload some of the excess inner energy.

This emotionally rooted pressure and tension can make it difficult for others to feel entirely relaxed in your company, although you are generally quite suspicious of people, and rarely allow easy access to the inner sanctum of your personal life, so this distancing tends to suit you. Domestically, you dislike intrusion, and take special offence at anyone attempting to dictate to you or patronise you; if anyone is going to be dominating and controlling, then it has to be you! Although you also tend to dictate and control your immediate family and anyone else that you can, you dislike having to acknowledge others in positions of authority. You can just about accept them if you feel they truly deserve their positions, but otherwise you show little respect and may even actively undermine their influence. It follows that you are never the ideal employee!

You can find it difficult to be consistent in your intimate relationships; not in the sense of loving, but more in the way in which you express it. This is due to the emotional blockages, and the need to retain control, and so you may appear to blow hot and cold to your partner; but this is a reflection upon how your inner emotional world is at any given time, rather than upon any questions of the depth of love you may feel.

You will be emotionally sensitive, and feel really hurt if the other does not respond to your advances, as you have a low threshold for pain on that level which amplifies your swings of mood. You tend to 'store pain', and this only increases the inner pressure over a period of time, which in turn affects your domestic relations, and so on, in a vicious circle. Frustration can occur as you expect much from your close relations and from life, and yet it is often triggered by your own inner problems causing you to receive and enjoy less than you should. Your whole contact with the outer world is feeling-orientated, and its impact upon you is always through your emotional body, which will colour your basic perception of life.

There may be disputes related to finances or inheritances in the family, and certainly over the positions of family authority, which you intend to win. You do not often welcome advice from others as you see it as interference or attempted domination, and you will invariably attempt to make your own decisions and tread your own path; even if it does appear to take you in the wrong direction, it is still your decision and choice, and in that sense it is right.

You will need to acknowledge the rights of others, and their importance in your life more. Again, compromise is a necessary virtue that you need to learn to apply, or through sheer hard-headedness and obstinacy you could lose more than you gain through lack of moderation and balance. Learn to value your partner, become less insistent upon your own will and desires and listen to others more; a little change in you could stimulate considerable benefits to emerge, ones which cost you far less than you imagine, and which do not really change you except for the better. They can also serve to drain away some of that emotional energy which at present you probably find is hard to deal with in a positive manner. Instead of trying to remake your family and close friends, turn the impulse inwards, and use it to remake yourself in a more socially harmonious image, as that is what Pluto is attempting to persuade you to achieve.

MERCURY–PLUTO ASPECTS

Mercury–Pluto Conjunction

You should have a powerful, penetrating and incisive mind, which is attracted towards delving deeply behind appearances. Whether these are social facades or intellectual theories or philosophies, your innate curiosity will enable you to look beneath the surface. As you tend to see your mind as a resource which you can utilise, you often collect many fragments of information on your searches, which you attempt to collate together into a workable source.

You feel 'at home' in your mind, enjoying applying it to a multitude of challenges and problems, confident in your ability to resolve them or make some kind of sense out of them. Following your natural investigative ability, you have an inner process occurring whereby you attempt to extract meaning from your studies and experience, hidden meanings that are mostly relevant only to yourself, although some may be of value to a wider audience too. There is a purist streak in your mind which prompts you to take quite an impersonal attitude to people and events, especially attaching a high value to 'truth' over the social games that people play; your directness is likely to stimulate reactions from others.

As usual with the Pluto energy, there will be an unknowable depth and dimension to your mind, with a tendency towards powerfully expressed extremism and assertiveness as you proceed to manifest your objectives. Your ability to concentrate your will-power and sustain it for as long as necessary will aid you in achieving your dreams. Your beliefs and opinions will tend to be fixed, and you will be difficult to shake from any position that you have decided to take, preferring a vigorous expression of your standpoint against any opponents. As you hate to be seen to have a weaker or fallacious argument, you tend to be well-prepared and confident upon any theme that you may be challenged upon; otherwise you have already prepared some way to evade a confrontation if you feel that you could be defeated. There may be a tendency to hold a grudge against any who have opposed you, or who stand in your way, and you will remember them, waiting for a suitable time to settle the scores.

Unnecessary social problems and suffering for people will draw out a sense of aggrieved anger in you, as will social and political hypocrisy. You will tend to respond to these feelings by becoming more involved in reorientating your energies into channels which directly oppose those who appear to be creating or amplifying such problems. You feel that you can contribute towards changing things for the better, and this can lead you towards involvement with radical politics. The nature of your political views will depend on your personal analysis of causes, but in extreme cases may tend towards anarchism. Any tactics of subversion will appeal to the Pluto energy, as will the emphasis upon change and transformation. If the social emphasis of Pluto dominates, then much of your life will be directed by the theme of transformation, social and political.

You will tend to be demanding in your personal relationships, expecting a high quality and strength from any partner. But even though you may attempt to force them to submit to you psychologically, it will be much better if you fail, for a good relationship needs equality and mutual respect. You often tend to use your persuasive power to influence others to agree with you, but you have to learn more tolerance and a broader understanding of the freedom and rights of others to hold their own views. Ideally your long-term partner should be similar to you in outlook, motivation and interests, because you may tend to turn the relationship into a form of intellectual power struggle, which would probably turn it sour before long if you did not have these in common. The obsessive tone of Pluto may cause some difficulties, both in your mental preoccupations, and in your relationship, especially if you are unaware of this aspect to yourself, which can easily turn you towards being excessively self-centred if unmoderated. The positive side of a relationship is that it can break down such tendencies, and open up the awareness of 'the other'; certainly you should learn to appreciate any relationship as bringing a more expansive quality into your life.

Mercury–Pluto Sextile

The nature of your mind will be biased towards intellectualism, and you will be attracted towards the realm of ideas, expressing a creative and questioning curiosity plus the ability to understand the variety of answers that you discover from various sources. Your mind will tend to be analytical, and you are likely to be attracted towards work which involves enquiry, research or teaching. You have the ability to intuit an underlying, synthesising cohesive meaning within the varied knowledge you acquire, and this can be shared with others. Your enthusiastic enquiring nature can stimulate others to search for answers themselves, without total reliance upon 'authorities'. You also tend to acquire considerable information about a large variety of subjects quite easily, retaining it in your memory, so that you can be a repository of entertaining or even important knowledge for the benefit of others.

Your mind will be penetrative and perceptive, often seeing through the appearances of things into their essential components, and new ideas and thinking will certainly hold fascination for you. The fact that you also have a vivid and creative imagination can help you to make new and interesting connections linking your knowledge into new patterns implying new understanding, perceptions and directions.

In your personal relationships, you tend to be straight and direct, and apart from expecting the same from others, you are unlikely to forget any who seem to live by lower standards and choose to be less honest in their contacts with you. Trust and honesty are very important to you, and you require both in any partnership. Basically, you will feel inwardly quite self-assured and secure, and your stability can be used as a support for others in times of trouble. You have an ability to mix naturally with a wide range of people, and value this broadening of contacts, as it serves to increase your storehouse of information. Usually, you are competent in dealing with your personal resources in an effective way, and should have no real difficulty in achieving a reasonable standard of living.

You may have to be wary of the tendency to believe that you are always right in your beliefs, opinions and knowledge; after all, nobody ever is, and you can blind yourself to this as you are quite an effective and fluent communicator who can often dominate an audience. You tend to back up your arguments by what appear to be unassailable facts and evidence, but you should be aware that in today's world, there is often a store of evidence and facts that contradicts your argument. As in most personal expressions, especially of opinions and beliefs, one should leave space within them to allow for change or alteration, to be ready to acknowledge other views and to be less dogmatic or obsessed by the personal need to be always right.

Mercury–Pluto Trine

The energy of the trine aspect can often be too 'rarified' to be fully used, as it is too subtle to be correctly grasped and applied by many people. Its natural affinity tends to be towards higher science or metaphysics, where the interface between mind and reality is explored and understood in terms of consciousness and energy. It relates more to a trained intellect working in spheres of abstract contemplation, or the connection between the intuitive flash of direct 'knowing' and the grounding through intellectual earthing in a pragmatic application.

In the everyday world, you will find that your main preoccupation will be with developing the ability to concentrate, to improve the use of your mind and ways of expressing yourself. Unless you are able to achieve the higher flights of this aspect, you will have to ground the energy in more mundane concerns, endeavouring to channel it by determined concentration. Otherwise, it tends to fly high and make you a little scatterbrained and mentally undisciplined.

The unknown will fascinate you though, and you will be curious to explore more, but ensure that you are fully grounded before commencing. You are likely to be quite inventive in your ideas, potentially quite creative if you have enough control over your mind to exploit them fully and effectively. The Mercury energy will give you analytical and investigative skills which can be turned to your advantage, but you will have to guard against the tendency to believe that you know it all.

You enjoy the challenge of competition, and you always intend to win. Failure leads you to brood and to scheme your next move, and here the Pluto energy implies manipulation to undermine your challengers; mentally, you can have a ruthless streak that people may not expect. You prefer full involvement and participation in things; you need to be interested enough so that a process of absorption can occur for a full experience, and if this is not happening, then your contribution rapidly dwindles to being less than zero, even becoming negative as you begin to look for ways out to find a new, more promising area to explore. You find it hard to motivate yourself in such a situation.

In personal relationships, you can be a little authoritarian, especially as you believe that you have a clear sense of 'right and wrong' and can become fixed in your attitudes. You are able to penetrate through social appearances into people, to sense their true attitudes and motives. This guides you in life, both to be wary of some, and to work with others whose genuine potential you are able to stimulate. This can lead to an involvement with co-ordinating groups where your energy serves both to stimulate new thinking and to open it out to new insights entering the group, or new ways of applying current ideas in practical application. You can be a little too mentally self-absorbed, and lack the sense of social concern and responsibility that the Pluto energy amplifies in most people who are responding to its lighter side.

Ideally, your personal partners should be basically similar in mind and attitude to yourself. This is because your energy qualities do not mix easily with opposite and conflicting views, and if you do enter into a relationship with someone of dissimilar views, then much time will be spent in direct confrontation, generally leading to its collapse. You will be willing to pour a lot of energy into a positive partnership, but you will also have high standards and expectations of your mate; choosing wisely is the key, through awareness of your own nature and knowledge of what is compatible with it.

Mercury–Pluto Square

The square can give you a harshness of temperament and expression, where your direct, blunt style can often create conflict and confrontation between yourself and others. Even though you prefer to reflect yourself as one capable of handling the 'real situation', you tend to lack a sensitivity towards possible reactions to your potentially penetrating insights. You rarely 'wrap' them up in socially acceptable packages for consumption, but offer them raw.

Your approach to life has a tendency to be extreme, a little suspicious of others' motives and intentions, secretive about your own, and basically pessimistic in tone. Your behaviour can often be unpredictable and erratic, making it difficult for others to take you for granted, and encouraging them to keep a certain distance away from you. You are a little uneasy with close contact in relationships, taking considerable time to develop a feeling of trust and relative relaxation with a partner. There is a tendency to try to manipulate and mould any partner so that they conform to your point of view, and often your views become intolerant and fixed, allowing little space for flexibility or change to occur naturally.

Sometimes, in an effort to achieve your own will, you rely upon your strong will-power to dominate others. Sometimes this can succeed, but you are equally liable to apply it incorrectly through a lack of proportion and through insensitivity, creating more damage to your aims and others than you intended. Similarly, whilst your choice of expressive style is straight and direct, you often devote much time towards scheming and plotting, which again, often works to your disadvantage.

In many ways, you project your own shadow qualities onto others, finding it hard to trust them, yet laying plots yourself; it is unlikely that you have any special ability to motivate others or to become a spokesperson for any group, as you are more of a loner. Towards authority you are ambivalent, making use of any power and authority that you may possess at home or work, yet being quite anti-authoritarian if you hold a low opinion of those responsible positions, particularly disliking a role under any domination by others.

Mentally, you require more self-discipline and understanding to make more positive use of your abilities of penetrative insight; in particular, the way in which you present yourself to others may need to be moderated. More control regarding your thoughts and words can help to avoid any controversy and unnecessary conflict with others, and a redirection of your powers of insight inward, so that you can observe how you are projecting those negative shadow qualities out onto others in the world when these qualities should be being internally transformed and the energies released for creative positive applications. Potentially, you have the sort of mind to absorb a variety of opposite views and arrive at a new synthesis of the essential values hidden within each of them, and then to express a unifying point or common ground from which dialogue can arise to resolve the apparent divisions. Such a talent could be extremely effective and important if the necessary inner changes are undergone and a redirection of your life results; a temporary phase which you may experience is the adoption of whichever view/belief system is currently in the forefront of your attention, but that at least can reveal flexibility and potential attitude change in you. Dissolving fixed barriers is possible, and the potential for change in your lifestyle and relationships is the main challenge that Pluto is facing you with.

Mercury–Pluto Opposition

The energy of the opposition aspect creates considerable inner pressure and tension, mentally and emotionally, and can be difficult to deal with constructively, as a considerable inner change is required before the energy can come under the control of an integrated personality.

Due to the inner agitation and anxiety, your perception of the world and your feeling response to events will be strongly coloured by its activity. This is not necessarily to imply that your interpretation is wrong, but that your experience of it will affect you more deeply and influentially than it would most other people, who could possibly give it more sense of proportion than you can. Basically, the tone of your insight will be pessimistic and essentially depressive, and you will see the world as a place where disorder, pain and problems are rapidly multiplying. Social problems feel personal and real to you, even if your own circumstances do not bring you into personal contact with them. Your sensitivity (or inner receptivity) leads you to see a world in crisis, makes you feel responsible for its problems, and offers little way out for you unless you become involved in efforts to improve matters. It is a 'social conscience writ large and painfully'. The frustrating thing for you is that however effective you are, so much work still needs to be done in the world. You have to accept the fact that you cannot change everything, and that your role is to make your own contribution but not everyone else's.

This sense of impatience in life creates a corresponding vibration in you that expresses itself as a brusque harshness in relating to others. The contradiction is that whilst you intend to improve life and bring harmony into people's relationships, you often create the opposite reaction to your purpose. An interrogatory style in talking to others will create distance, and under pressure of your 'mission' you often lose sight of co-operative relationship with others. You need to learn more compromise and moderation, paying equal attention to the needs and feelings of co-workers or partners. Gain a truer perspective on the conditions of time, and the slowness of change in the world, and this can help to moderate your impatience at social transformation; it is a long, slow grind against inertia and resistance, often even from those you believe you are helping.

You have high ideals, yet are often lacking in self-confidence over your ability to express them or live up to them; generally, no one can live up to high ideals, so relax a little, create a little space between you and this inner obsession, and devote more time to internalising this energy to transform yourself. What you are is of the highest importance, and by embodying your ideal more fully in yourself, you will be more of a living demonstration of your purpose, and more effective.

It is a difficult tension to live with, this feeling of interrelatedness with the world, a sense of responsibility and direction that you are 'summoned' to give aid to lighten the burden. You have to lighten your own burden first, which will improve the quality of your own life immensely, and bring clarity and perspective into things.

VENUS–PLUTO ASPECTS

Venus–Pluto Conjunction

Your intimate personal relationships will be extremely important in your life, creating a sphere of experience which can take you to both the heights and depths of emotional intensity, and will be a focus for energies of transformation which will influence the direction of your life.

What you are searching for is 'the ultimate physical/emotional affair' a consuming passionate emotional involvement with your ideal partner, and this desire will play a prominent role in your choices of partner for relationship. Unfortunately, what you are chasing is more of an illusion rather than a reality, a dream figure projected from your own psyche that you look to find in the objective world; the anima and animus images of Jungian psychology. As real life has a habit of shattering illusions, you will often be frustrated in your relationships, which could lead you to experiment with a variety of partners, none of whom seem to fit your inner picture of 'perfection'.

Emotionally, you can be difficult to satisfy, as you tend to believe that there is always a greater intensity and experience that has so far eluded you, but which would be within your reach if only you could find the right partner. Inevitably, your emotional life will be full of highs and lows, and the likelihood is that you will either break up promising relationships or allow them to fall apart by withdrawing your commitment, because you are already casting your net for a more suitable mate. It can be difficult for someone who is emotionally attached to you, as you tend to 'blow hot and cold', fire, passion and intensity, and ice, distance and disinterest as your partner displays their more frail human face. Only a 'god or a goddess' will do for you!

The point is that you are externalising your inner ideal partner, and what is required is that you realise that you have to evoke these qualities from within your own nature, to become more complete and self-sufficient in yourself, rather than look for another to bear the strain of expressing them, and upon whom you lean. You have to reabsorb your own fantasy projection, stop expecting another to live up to your ideal, and learn how to embody it yourself. It is a step in moving towards the inner androgynous state of being, where the physical male integrates his anima, allowing 'traditional female qualities' of sensitivity, intuitiveness, nurturing and caring to enrich his life, and the physical woman integrates her animus, releasing qualities of action, intellect and assertiveness to enrich her life; an inner balance.

Until you begin to make progress in this inner psychological necessity then it is likely that you will continue to find an underlying dissatisfaction in your relationships, a feeling that there must be more somewhere. You need to change in order to create an opportunity for your relationships to stand a chance of working; you need to accept the real nature of people, their weaknesses and strengths and learn to love real flesh and blood people. Potentially, your capacity for the intensity of love can stimulate considerable transformation in yourself and partners, acting as a healing and development catalyst; the process of rebirth in your life will come via your emotions, but be prepared to suffer the 'death of the heart' first.

Your vitality and energy can give you an artistic temperament and ability, coupled with a style of dramatic self-expression, and people will rarely respond to you in a lukewarm manner, finding themselves either strongly attracted to the consuming flame or repulsed as the intensity is too much for them. Transformation, perhaps through the reorientation of your excess vital emotional energy towards a spiritual or social cause, could help regeneration, offering equal intensity but from a stabilised inner balance.

Venus–Pluto Sextile

The sextile aspect is an easier one to experience than the conjunction or the challenging square and opposition. The state of a more harmonious inner balance is easier to find, and there is a more realistic appreciation and understanding of the nature of human love and relationships.

The experience of your feelings and emotions will be strong, but will be able to be absorbed into a personal integration rather than be a compulsive dominating energy driving the life. This means that you should be able to gain some perspective upon the patterns of your emotional life, to see the rhythmic cycle, and to apply common sense, logic and rationality to moderate any obsessive tendencies emanating from that level.

Understanding is a key for you, and you have an insight into the potentially transformative and beneficial power of love in human life. To you, having a successful intimate relationship is a high priority, although you will tend to be very careful in your choice of partners. What you require is a partner who is capable of developing with you, as the relationship matures and changes over time, where there is a natural love and respect for each other, mutual or compatible interests and where both will benefit from each other's company. Running though the partnership will be a thread of purpose and meaning, perhaps a joint life direction to be aimed towards, which is nourished by a high degree of real communication and sharing. Your ideals are high, but are achievable in real life; the key to success lies in right mutual choice, and this can come about through a series of events that could imply that the partnership is 'fated' to occur. Feeling this way can give a strength and inner commitment to the relationship at those times when mutual adjustment and personal change are required for the relationship to progress and deepen over the years.

Sexuality will be important to you, but not compulsively so, as you will see it as a natural, enjoyable aspect of adult life, and are unlikely to have any damaging feelings of unease about physical expressions of love and affection. Talents in the arts or music are at least latent in you, and if you draw these out strongly enough, you may discover that you have quite an original creative ability to display.

Venus–Pluto Trine

The trine aspect gives similar indications to the sextile, where the possibility of personal transformation is likely to occur through emotional experiences of a higher and intense kind.

You will have a fundamental faith in life, an innate optimism that all will work out well in the end. This belief in the goodness of life can be 'contagious', and you may feel attracted towards sharing with others your personal approach or philosophy of life, so that they too can experience how trust, faith and love can enrich and guide a life. You feel that higher values are essential in interpersonal relationships, and you try to embody these in your own life. You see that the bedrock of a partnership – apart from mutual love and affection – lies in qualities of commitment, honesty, integrity, responsibility to mutual obligations, and allowing each other the space to express his or her own unique nature and to continue to unfold the personality in a developmental way. Generally, you have a belief that the lives of others could be greatly improved if certain adjustments were made in their attitudes, and you are probably correct in assuming so. You may, however, have to avoid a tendency to interfere in the choices that others make. They have to find their own way, although you have the potential to help others do this, perhaps by encouraging them to examine themselves and their options.

You should have a sense of life direction to follow, a meaningful path which may appear in hindsight to have an element of inevitability about it. Similarly, your intimate love life may feel preordained, and you may find that you are waiting for that special partner to enter your life, not feeling quite right with any previous relationships or fully able to commit yourself to them. It could be that you experience the right partner in the traditional sense of 'love at first sight', an intuitive feeling of 'rightness'.

Whether immediately obvious or not, your life will be strongly directed and influenced by your emotions; your choices will always be conditioned by your emotional responses to people and situations, even though you may overlay your 'gut reaction' by intellectual reasons or logic. Fortunately, your choices tend to turn out right for you, unlike the choices made by those with the Venus–Pluto square or opposition, where following emotional impulses leads towards considerable difficulties and frustrations.

It may be that some of the higher appreciation and
potentially are yours to experience, may remain lat
are triggered into conscious activity through the tr
action of love upon you; meeting your 'fated partne
stimulus for this process. This does not necessarily i
relationship will succeed and survive, but could in
and turning-point in your life centred within yo
which – whatever the result – will lead to enhanced u
and inner change.

Venus–Pluto Square

Pluto introduces an element of fate into your emo
which are likely to be a source of problems in yo
intense emotions are liable to dictate the nature of
and you may experience difficulties through bei
control your desires and passions. This can inv
relationships that may be basically unsuitable, and w
stimulate aspects of your character that may not be t
your partner's benefit. At an extreme, such relatio
become mutually destructive and life-spoiling, or de
debasement of character.

Social and materialistic conditions will tend to i
potential fulfilment, and you are likely to be attracted towards those who seem to offer money, possessions and social status as well as a personal relationship. This is partly because of your need for a sense of security, and it can play a deciding factor in your affairs or marriage. Conversely, in the inebriation of passion, you may find that you are committed to someone who has none of these additional 'assets', and that the lack of them eventually has a negative effect on the relationship.

You are probably too self-centred in relationship, eagerly taking but giving less in return, and yet discovering that you are still not experiencing the peaks of emotional and sexual intensity that you imagine are there; this builds a feeling of frustration over time, which dissipates much of your ability to enjoy and causes you to begin a process of withdrawal from your commitment and responsibility, mentally, emotionally and physically.

A conflict that you encounter is that of chasing your desires, or chasing your needs. You may need to spend some time actually deciding what your real *needs* actually are, as opposed to *desires* – which are much less essential to your well-being. Experience should show you that there is usually a cost for everything, and that the fulfilment of genuine needs tends to bring in its wake far fewer negatives than does the compulsion to satisfy desires. One can imagine an infinite number of desires, but in general only a handful of needs demand to be met in order for one to enjoy life. It is your choice which you direct your energy towards. Chasing desires often encourages you to attempt to manipulate others through some form of personal domination

Crises associated with relationship and emotions are likely, providing you with the possibility of transformation and understanding of the energies of love, emotion and sex within yourself. This can break down your self-preoccupation, making you able to give and compromise more with your partner, to resolve the dangers of negative relationship and to have more conscious control over your strong impulsive drives and desires. One way to channel this energy is in artistic expression, as you should discover that you possess some talent in that area which may be lying latent. You should try to avoid any tendency towards entering secret love affairs, which, whilst they may stoke the fires of passion, also stimulate your more negative characteristics of not always being trustworthy and not always fulfilling your obligations.

Venus–Pluto Opposition

The challenging aspects of square and opposition invariably display the dark face of the distorted Pluto energy, and require considerable individual transformation and self-understanding to mitigate the potentially negative impact on life that they will otherwise influence a person to experience. It is important to remember that this influence to confront the darker side of the psyche is inherently positive and creatively beneficial if it is used to reorientate the inner life, and that this is the hidden purpose of the Pluto impulses.

It is likely that you will experience a repetitive pattern of sexual love and emotional affairs which either do not seem to satisfy and fulfil you, or which collapse into failure, acrimony and suffering. This can lead to a jaded, cynical attitude founded upon a frustrated, demoralised emotionally battered perception of love.

Your emotional intensity and passion is likely to cause difficulties for you, as it often seems to run away out of your control, and can take you into situations and encounters which from a clearer perspective you could consider to be undesirable. Certainly you are looking for something, but your sexual and emotional desires can be too strong, creating distortions of inner energy and leading to compulsive behaviour on your part – followed by an attempt at justification in the vein of 'I couldn't help myself . . .'. You will either feel driven to experiment in various relationships on a continuous basis, or as a reaction, you may attempt to avoid entering any emotional affair as you are afraid of experiencing the old established pattern again.

Problems can arise in your intimate relationships due to your tendency to introduce the element of domination. You tend to demand your own way or assume a dominating role, sometimes played out in potentially damaging sexual and emotional contexts, sometimes obvious, sometimes more subtle. Even if you assume a submissive role, it is only as a hidden way to manipulate and achieve your intentions through a subtle route; it is not your natural approach. Usually, you want your partners to change to suit you, and you can put intense pressure upon them, especially sexually and emotionally.

You will need to learn the necessity for mutual compromise in relationships, to understand your inner underlying desires and impulses which are conditioning and controlling you from the depths of your unconscious. It may be appropriate to study humanistic psychology, or take part in a course or therapy designed to bring about safe release of hidden impulses into the light of conscious awareness. Such impulses, and unconscious inner fantasy lives are present to some degree in everyone, but with this aspect they will stimulate problems for you, which are resolvable if you are willing to confront them in an act of personal reintegration and transformation. This will also serve to balance out your erratic flow of emotional desires, which often seems to confuse you and any partner, as you appear to 'blow very hot and very cold' in your responses to them; this is when your inner impulses arise and fall in some hidden rhythmic cycle, leading to uncontrollable emotional and sexual needs and intensity, or to a lack of response and coldness.

Always, the choice is yours; potentially you can defuse many of the difficulties that usually face you in relationships, or you can continue hoping that they will lift of their own accord. Pluto is influencing you to take the positive approach, by facing you with the results of being passive to the inner forces and by remaining unconscious of their hidden promptings.

MARS–PLUTO ASPECTS

Mars–Pluto Conjunction

This aspect should give you considerable physical energy and vitality which you can apply to tasks requiring persistence, determination and endurance. You are able to direct a potent will towards realising your aims, and your innate vitality when rightly directed will be the means by which you steer your life course.

The energy can tend to amplify any self-centred tendencies in you, stimulating your desire nature and setting goals to achieve which would be primarily for your own personal benefit and satisfaction. You may like to create challenges for yourself, as a test for the efficacy of your 'powers'. If this tendency is allowed to dictate life choices, then you may become dominated by an insatiable desire compulsion, which is rarely fulfilled; this can reflect a certain naivety or innocence in your outlook which is essentially selfish and adolescent in quality, and the 'I want' syndrome may need more conscious moderation in order for you to regain control.

Often you will prefer to assert your individuality, sometimes even as a compulsive expression despite the reactions of others. You may not always think things through enough, or consider the possible implications of your actions and words prior to committing yourself. This can obviously create some difficulties for you; it is similar to the behaviour of an adolescent, which as most parents discover can lead to considerable family friction.

You will have a dislike of restrictions imposed upon you, always having a need for as much freedom as possible. If you feel that your energy is imprisoned, then you will be looking for the way out, feeling that before too long your energy will explode, and this can be quite uncomfortable. To minimise this, you should try to develop your life so that your choices of partner and work are reasonably compatible with your needs, if only to avoid unnecessary inner friction.

In your intimate relationships, you may be too forceful and aggressive. The Pluto energy will tend to make you too possessive and demanding of a partner, and you may attempt to dominate by your sexual expression. Sexual experiences will hold great meaning for you, and you will try to release much of your physical vigour on the physical level in an intense and potentially transforming manner. You may need to gain greater control over this aspect of yourself, to avoid it becoming obsessive or too extreme and violent in approach or tone.

As you mature more, you may discover an increasing interest in and awareness of social concerns, and this can be a fruitful channel through which to express your vitality and talents. You can be quite useful in encouraging others to apply their positions of power and influence to work for greater social benefit, and your ability to resolve difficult situations by strength of will can be creatively positive.

Mars–Pluto Sextile

You will expect honesty and straightforwardness in your dealings with people, preferring to hear the truth rather than be confused by evasion, innuendo and psychological manipulation. In fact truthfulness is one of your most highly valued qualities. You have a sensitivity to the motives of others, and whilst you have no real illusions about the nature of the human race, you tend to give a high regard to the principle of truth, whilst maintaining a wary eye on your fellow men. You cannot always live up to your own ideal, but at least you try!

You have a mind which tends to be analytical and deductive. Added to this, you are articulate and generally persuasive – if only in the force with which you express your opinions, arguments and beliefs – and have a grasp of dramatic presentation which you apply in order to influence listeners in your favour, personally and to support your position.

Your level of physical vitality should be high, and you may be attracted towards exploiting your body or developing it in terms of physical activity and culture. You should have a more healthy and positive approach to sexual expression than those who have the Mars–Pluto square or opposition, and you perceive sex in essentially natural terms without inner compulsions complicating and distorting the energy release.

Usually, others know where you stand on things, as you are not shy of revealing your viewpoints, and express them clearly and directly, and you expect the same from others. If people tend to express themselves in less direct ways, and if you later discover them to have been telling lies, then you can be quite unforgiving in your attitude to them; even if you store the knowledge away for reference, they have forfeited your total trust.

You may need to become a little less self-righteous. Because of

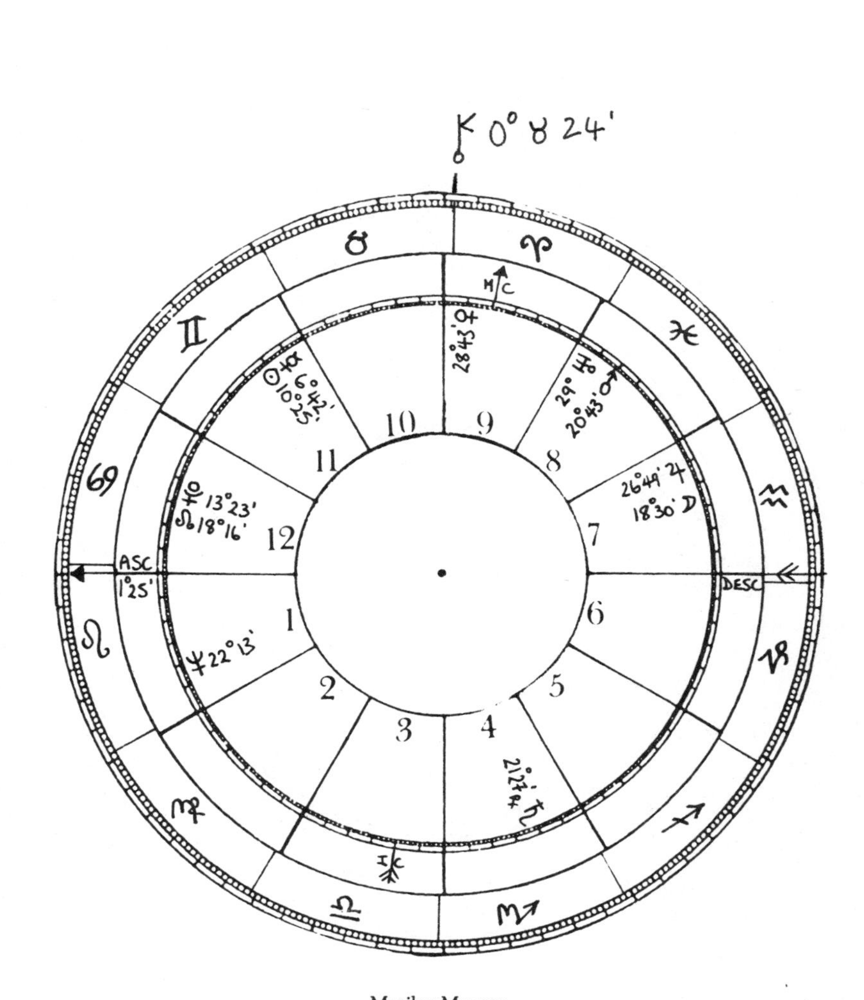

Marilyn Monroe
Film actress
archetypal 'star'
Pluto Trine Mars
Natal Pluto 12th House

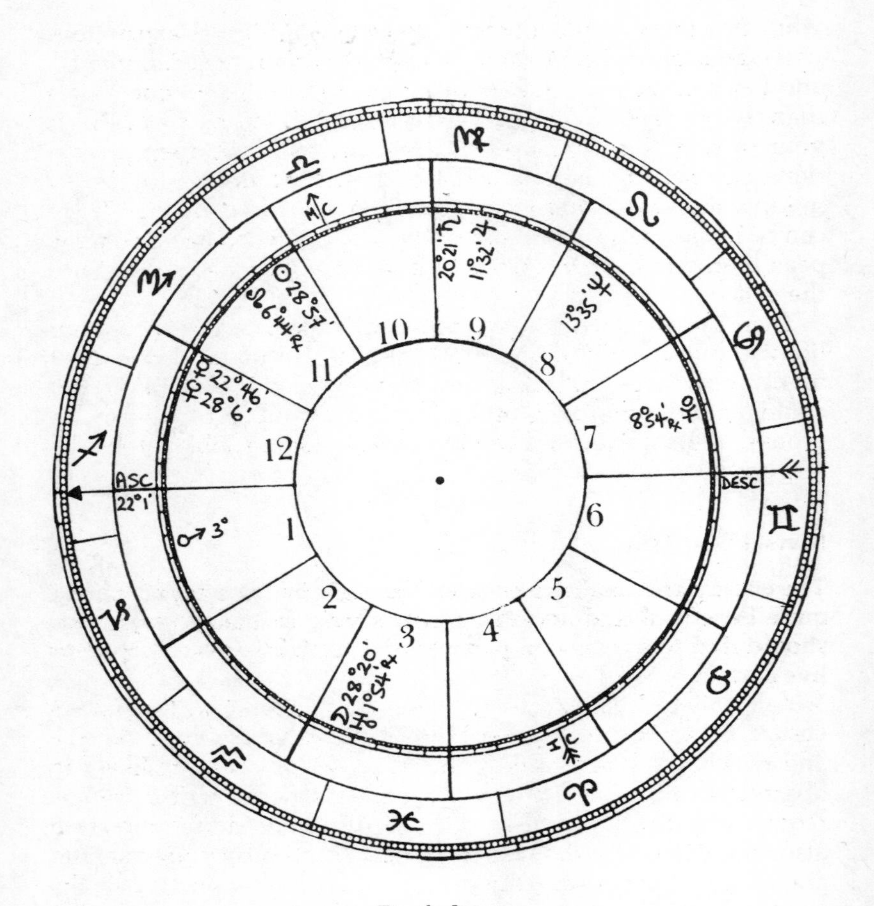

Timothy Leary
Visionary, futurist,
LSD High Priest of the
'60s
Pluto Sextile Jupiter
Pluto Oppositon Mars
Pluto Trine Uranus
Natal Pluto 7th House

your directness, forcefulness and relative clarity of expression, you may begin to believe that your perception is invariably right, and begin to pay more attention to your own pronouncements than to the views of others. The viewpoint of others is as valid as your own, and is usually worth listening to, as different perceptions can help to expand your own understanding, to correct misapprehensions, and to enhance contact and dialogue. There can be many routes to the top of the mountain and even from the peak there can be many ways to reflect the view back down into the valley.

There may be a tendency to think and talk about things in your life without actually doing them, almost as though this level of involvement were sufficient and satisfying. It is likely that you could manifest your aims in a more distinct and objective way, to ground them more in everyday reality and enable others to respond to and share them.

Mars–Pluto Trine

The energy and qualities released through the trine aspect can be quite beneficial and socially constructive. In many ways, you should find this an uncomplicated and straightforward aspect to live and work with.

You will feel at ease in applying your potent will-power to ensure the success of any aims that you clearly decide to achieve and which are realistically within your scope. You are likely to observe over time that, when necessary, the self-discipline required to direct your will consistently in the chosen direction also stimulates an inner change to occur, whereby your qualities and talents seem to be remixed or rebalanced according to the needs of your objectives. This can be very useful as a regeneration of the inner life to reflect a pattern of internal harmony, in which conflicting energies and tendencies are no longer competing for expression and diverting your attention away from your purpose. However, this process should only occur during phases where you need to be intensely one-pointed and concentrated enough to make your decisive active step, and should not be encouraged to continue, as the result may be a repression of aspects of your personality and a pushing them down into the unconscious mind. See it as a temporary 'selective tightening' necessary for a short time and then allow a relaxation and a release of these temporarily unexpressed aspects to be free again in your personality.

You tend to have insight into people and situations, and the capacity for direct, realistic analysis. You prefer to allow space for others to be themselves, being quite tolerant of most people – providing they are not causing deliberate harm or taking advantage of others. In addition, you have a clear sense of interrelationship with society, and feel that you have a natural responsibility to use your energies in a socially constructive way. In particular, you take a certain pleasure in attempting to resolve social problems by becoming involved with social pressure groups which indicate directions to follow which they believe would be socially beneficial. You can become very committed to supporting causes that you have faith in, devoting time and energy to furthering the cause, and in being true to yourself and your personal beliefs. The only point to bear in mind with such a tendency, is the need for an ongoing evaluation of belief and self, to determine your current standpoint and to allow it to change and evolve naturally, as you develop through time and greater life experience; belief should not be an unquestioning, static position.

Mars–Pluto Square

With the energy released by the square, you will be mainly motivated by self-centred tendencies and a need to 'throw out' overflowing and excess martian energy. You tend to think that the power of your natural energy is sufficient to win you success and satisfaction, and indeed the force and directness of it often can, but using it in such a way often overrides sensitivity and awareness of others. Considered aims and planning are often ignored under the immediacy of impulse and desire, and a spirit of recklessness can ignore any thoughts of the possible future consequences of your actions, provided you believe that your desires will be satisfied.

You find it difficult to motivate yourself for long periods of time, as in a commitment to achieve something through careful planning; you have problems in disciplining and directing your will sufficiently for that kind of effort, and you are more suited to using your force in a more immediate, spontaneous impulse for self-satisfaction. This is also partly because you experience some conflict in directing your will to achieve your desires, and rarely feel as though you are making the most of your talents.

There can be a sense of inner frustration, caused by the forceful nature of this energy, and a lack of a suitable channel along which to direct it in a constructive manner. This will create a lack of patience, a potentially violent temper and sexual aggressiveness, where you 'throw out' excess energy through a dictatorial and demanding personality in order to dominate others. You may need to develop a more healthy perspective on sexual expression, one which regards sex more in terms of relationship and partnership, and less in terms of self-satisfaction, energy release, domination, exploitation and aggressiveness.

This experience of inner stress is symptomatic of clashing energies; it is not something that you have to endure all your life; it can be adjusted to be more harmonious. One way to begin this reorientation is to learn how to determine the overall direction of your life, to see a broader picture of your immediate social influence and how you want to live in relationship with others. To break down this preoccupation with self and to appreciate and acknowledge the feelings and needs of others as being as valid as your own is essential, and a key to transformation. By becoming clearer as to personal aims, you can begin to apply your will consistently in order to achieve them over time; desires for instant self-gratification are unrealistic. Learn how to live in equality of partnership and relationship; a mutuality of needs, desires and responsibilities requires mutual sharing and co-operation. Avoid tendencies towards domination and power struggles. Basically, you require suitable channels into which to pour your energy, constructive channels that are life-enhancing for you and others. You tend to devote most time and energy in opposing others through conflict and aggression rather than in working together for group benefit; find ways to become positively in favour of something, and then add your energy to help it become real. There is much greater satisfaction and fulfilment in that form of achievement than struggling to satisfy a very separate self that you try to maintain.

Mars–Pluto Opposition

The opposition aspect tends to reflect an inner conflict in you, that of a clash between your personal desires and a possible contributing positive role in society, as represented by the opposition between the personal Mars desires and the more socially orientated Pluto.

You probably require a greater understanding of the nature of personal power, the right application of it to benefit the group rather than to satisfy purely personal aims and desires, especially as you may have the tendency to take advantage of a group's power and influence to further your own ambitions.

Your nature will express a forceful will, which can be experienced by others as aggressiveness, making them avoid too close a contact with you; in fact, you often appear to be quite unaware of your effect on people, and a greater sensitivity to the rights and reality of others is a quality that you could do well to help develop. This would help to minimise any negative effect you may have on others, especially those in close relationship to you, whom you often attempt to dominate. Control in an intimate context is attractive to you, and you are likely to have an intense and powerful sexual nature, which at times can lead towards an affinity with forms of potentially violent passion and sexual undertones. You tend to link sex with power as an exaltation of personal force, and this can stimulate certain problems, although some potential partners can find the sheer physicality extremely exciting and provocative. This, plus the psychological manipulation that you attempt, can lead to stormy relations, and you are probably wiser to moderate and discipline your release of energy through a controlled awareness of its impact on others. You may observe that your flow of sexual energy can be erratic and irregular, where your passions are either 'hot' or very 'cold', and you are basically unable to regulate them according to demand or switch them on.

In your home life, you may find problems arising in the spheres of financial management, power struggles, and on the emotional levels of relationships. You probably find that your emotions are driven by the force of passion and sexual energy, and that you have a lack of real understanding of their nature, as they tend to be swept along on the tide. Perhaps this is why you often demonstrate little awareness of the emotions of others in everyday life, as yours are often held in a state of suspended repression, like waters blocked from following their natural route by a dam wall. If the emotional level was released carefully and consistently in a healthy way, the blocked Pluto energy operating on that level could be freed, and many of your problems would begin to dissolve, leading to personal transformation. This would then adjust the level of force and suppressed violence in you, so that you would deal with your power more positively. This would lead to a clearer perception of self and others, allowing partners more personal freedom through mutual agreement and compromise, rather than your previous imposition of will. Taking such a course could develop also towards greater social involvement, using your energy in positive and creative channels, realising that if you can change from living mainly to satisfy purely personal desires at the expense of others, then there is the potential for a self-centred violent society to change from exploitation to co-operation and mutual benefit.

JUPITER–PLUTO ASPECTS

Jupiter–Pluto Conjunction

This is a favourable aspect, which should allow you the opportunity to unfold your natural talents relatively easily, applying them in a concentrated and determined approach towards achieving your ambitions. You have the fortunate ability to evoke a response from your 'inner storehouse' of gifts, and create an open channel enabling you to manifest these in an objective context. Those who are close to you or who work daily with you may be inspired by this ability, and you are likely to display certain leadership qualities.

You will approach life with zest and vitality, pouring your energy wholeheartedly into satisfying your aims and your need for success. You seem to feel that your success is guaranteed, and whilst you may often feel impatient, or temporarily frustrated in your purpose, you have too much self-confidence and determination to believe that you could fail. The opportunities are certainly there for you, and your inner gifts are there to be actively expressed and exploited by you to achieve success.

You may find that you express and explore your talents in several potentially lucrative areas, as your gifts can be applicable in a variety of ways. This can mean that you are likely to change direction several times throughout your life, possibly in a radical style, or just to find new areas to experience. You may not have a specific goal in mind – such as a senior managerial position in one company – but could become influenced by 'the inner storehouse' of innate talents to search for new directions in order to find suitable channels of release for as yet latent gifts; you may even find a problem arising out of the very multiplicity of choices available to you.

Ideally, you should look for a way of life which actually offers you a variety of channels through which to express yourself, where there is a potential for a renewal of challenges and for a demand of personal growth. Working closely with people is likely to attract you, and interpersonal relationships can be a constant sphere of creativity and growth; much can be shared and transmitted even in creating and maintaining positive human relations at work.

In an intimate relationship, you should ensure that equality is developed, building a balance, as you may have a tendency to play the role of dominating leader too often. Development of each partner is also important, and your partner's needs and abilities should be clearly recognised and valued, helping each other to actualise hidden potentials. Change in the relationship and in your partner should arise naturally and easily; never attempt to force any process, as a natural evolution is safest, especially when in truth you cannot really understand the inner process and life experience/perception of another.

The best use of your abilities will be towards benefiting others in some way. Whilst Pluto is likely to 'co-operate' with you using this energy for personal success, if you tend to apply it in a way that exploits or abuses others through your becoming obsessed with self-satisfaction and desires, you may find that Pluto becomes more subversive and undermines your purposes, stimulating failure as a natural result of your own distorted form of expression, thus creating your own downfall as Pluto forces you to look at the need for transformation.

Jupiter–Pluto Sextile

The sextile aspect gives a 'higher turn of the spiral' to the energy which is released, and this will enhance your mental and intuitional faculties. You will have an optimistic and positive outlook on life, and the way in which you and others will benefit is through the exploration of higher ideals, elevated ideas and philosophies or religions. This is the direction to travel towards, both as a form of self-discovery and unfoldment, and as a medium through which you can eventually express your insights and understanding back into the world for the use of others.

The potential is there for you to serve as a spiritual channel and transmitter, provided you ensure that you truly work for the good of humanity. Pluto will support any efforts you make to communicate a unified vision to the world, greatly enhancing the effectiveness of your influence. This real effectiveness will be determined by your ability to serve selflessly, either as an enunciator of a vision, or by a lifetime of support and co-operation with others who also seek to promote a positive direction for humanity to aim towards. There is no real glamour in such a task.

You have a penetrative mind and intuition, enabling you to discern the reality behind social, cultural and personal appearances, and there is a motivating curiosity that seems to require satisfying in whichever direction it turns. Your ideals are high, perhaps unrealistic to some degree, but still something to aspire towards in yourself and in the world. You are self-motivated and inspired, attempting to live to a high moral code (albeit your own), and tend to expect high ethical behaviour from those in positions of authority and social responsibility; hypocrisy and injustice you strongly object to. You will give your support to those whom you feel are being treated harshly and unfairly by society, and may often associate yourself with social and world movements to initiate change. Your sense of responsibility is highly developed, and you experience a strong inner impulse to share in the work of world regeneration and rebirth. Any close partnership should ideally involve someone who has a similar way of perceiving and experiencing the world, and it is quite possible that you could work together on projects, sharing a common ideal.

Jupiter–Pluto Trine

As with the sextile aspect, the trine indicates the potential of releasing a powerful creative energy emerging from a humanistic and spiritual perspective, which will be of positive use to yourself and the world.

Your innate optimism and belief in the essential goodness of life will turn your inner faith into an effective ability to manifest your creative vision, especially as you are able to channel your will into constructive forms of expression.

Your contribution to society may well be in working closely with people, and you have the gift of being able to inspire others to discover how to experience life more intensely and creatively and to release their own latent talents. This can involve you in the expression of a sort of life philosophy which can be adopted by others on their path to self-understanding. Obviously, any such influence must be carefully handled by you, both in how your own self-perception is changed and in what you offer to others or share with them. There is a great responsibility to be assumed when presenting yourself in a way that can have considerable influence upon others' lives, and awareness must be shown and applied to ensure integrity is maintained, that the 'teaching' is as honest and valid as possible, that there is freedom for disagreement or new thinking to occur, and that it is understood that 'your way' is not the only or most appropriate way for everyone. In fact, even direct opposition from another may be the right way for them to unfold themselves or to discover new insights, and could be right for you as a stimulus to re-evaluate your own path and attitudes.

Primarily, you seem to function in a role of 'educator', and you are likely to develop into an effective speaker, clearly expounding your beliefs, ideas and attitudes, and being quite persuasive in that way. You tend to need personal freedom, and dislike being tied down into predictable patterns of behaviour, as you may feel that you need to be relatively free in order to be able to respond to what you consider to be insights and intuitions. You support social transformation, and will reflect the unified vision as the direction for the future, offering a meaning and inspiring purpose for people to aim towards. You may find that a personal transformation is required of you prior to you fulfilling your potential role and function. Initially, this could involve considerable challenges facing you which require overcoming, or elements in your personal life that lead to periodic crises which lead eventually to wisdom and insight as a result of personal suffering.

Jupiter–Pluto Square

This indicates that your personal philosophy and attitudes will condition your life, and because they tend to be fixed and dogmatic can serve to bring you into conflict with others. This philosophy or set of beliefs will be either 'self-created' or tend to reflect older, more traditional religious dogma; either of them is likely to be out of phase with much of contemporary life and social development. You will either express a peculiarly unique and personally individual outlook, or be willingly absorbed within a traditional structure.

Basically, you are likely to be antagonistic to the modern world, believing that it is taking the wrong direction, and will be inclined towards a desire to reform the outer world and people so that they begin to conform to your world vision. There is a tendency towards mental arrogance, a certainty of your own way being right as opposed to the ways of others, and you are unlikely to be receptive to alternative beliefs and new ideas. You will be an active exponent of your way, expressing it forcefully to others, either by a challenging of their beliefs or by attempts at conversion; you feel that you have a mission to perform, and this conviction gives you the inner strength to continue. If rejection occurs, you tend not to use that experience as a means to re-evaluate your beliefs, but inwardly reassert your own sense of righteousness. Whilst it may appear that your system of belief is intellectually founded, the truth is that it is rooted deep in your emotions, and you feel its personal meaning very intensely, thus whilst attempting to challenge and persuade others, you maintain a barrier to outer challenges against yourelf. You are afraid that if your belief structure cracked and began to fall apart, then your inner cohesiveness as a personality would too, as your identity is so intertwined with your own beliefs.

To some degree, most people are in a similar situation to yourself, where self-identity is defined by beliefs, opinions, attitudes, thoughts, emotions and body; in defending personal convictions you are defending yourself. It may be that your particular belief is not obviously religious; it could easily be political: for many, a firmly held political conviction acts inwardly as a substitute 'god'.

You are attracted to power and influence, as a means to convert others and to confirm the efficacy of your own beliefs through personal success. What you may need to achieve is a way to co-operate with people more effectively, rather than attempting to dominate. Certainly, it may be wiser for you to allow a cross-fertilisation between yourself and the world, to dissolve the tendency towards fanatical closed-mindedness.

Jupiter–Pluto Opposition

You are liable to experience conflict arising from a tendency to try to be authoritative and dominant in respect of the beliefs and attitudes of others. Whilst you may often oppose contemporary values and social ethics and philosophy, challenging existing authorities by the power of your own convictions, what you are attempting to achieve is to influence others to accept and follow your own views, weaning them from one source of authority only to replace it with your own. This will probably be expressed in the spheres of politics, religion or philosophy.

Whilst you may feel that you have a 'duty' to express your own perception of things (which in terms of self-expression is fine), there are likely to be underlying personal motivations at work, which reflect personal ambitions for power over people or financial accumulation. Certainly, you see your form of assertive expression as a means to achieve greater personal social elevation; to become an authoritative leader in a context that appears to validate the rightness of your beliefs. You are not a natural follower, and find it difficult to work as a supporter in a group unless you are intending to become its leading light as soon as possible.

It is likely that your goals will be frustrated, partly because of the nature of your relationships with others, which may lack harmony due to your tendency towards an assertiveness that clashes with the equally held views of others. Others who need to follow stronger personalities may support you if you appear to be successful, but it is unlikely that you will have real respect for them and may easily attempt to exploit their support. Sometimes, it appears that you are reluctant to learn from your mistakes, as though obsessed by a belief in your own infallibility.

You tend to expect much from life, almost as your due rather than as the result of your own efforts, and yet you may have problems in fully applying yourself to succeed in your intentions. You may then blame others or mysterious circumstances for your lack of success rather than evaluate your own contribution and character. You are ambivalent about responsibility, trying to rise to positions of responsibility yet being reluctant to shoulder any yourself. This is because you wish to remain free to be spontaneous, able to move in any direction and respond to any desire that possesses you, without consideration for any influence it may have upon others in the future. This undisciplined side can lead to erratic and unpredictable behaviour, especially if you react against tensions and pressures arising from problems that you prefer to ignore or run away from instead of facing them determined to resolve them in a satisfactory manner. This can apply especially in close relationships, which you may tend to break rather than confront basic challenges.

Much of your direction is a result of an attempt to run away from the necessity for an inner reorientation, where your energies are used to remake yourself rather than trying to impose them upon others. Aiming outwards will lead to increasing frustration, through being undermined by the Pluto energy, and until you begin to look inwards at your own motives, tendencies and needs, it is unlikely that the outer world will bend sufficiently to your will. Co-operation, not opposition, will need to be developed, plus a willingness to listen to people and work with them without manipulative motives in group endeavours. Efforts in this direction will help to release your energy into more harmonious channels, and to dissolve the barriers that this aspect creates in yourself and with others.

SATURN–PLUTO ASPECTS

Saturn–Pluto Conjunction

Saturn implies restrictions and limitations, which serve as a barrier to progress until certain changes are made or lessons learnt, and when in association with Pluto, the way forward is conditioned by the need for an inner transformation to occur. With this aspect, it is likely that you will experience some degree of frustration in achieving your objectives, or a sense of invisible blockages facing you that require you to discover some way to pass them or dissolve them through penetration.

As you have a strong ambitious nature, you will need to make full use of all the resources available to you, applying accumulated knowledge and experience to a determined persistent effort to succeed. Patience will be an essential quality for you to develop, as it is unlikely that you will have rapid immediate success in your objectives. Usually you have to wait, and undergo the experience of frustration and not knowing if your goals will be realised, and this can be a testing and transformative phase, especially as it is likely to be repeated periodically throughout your life.

You will be attracted towards power and status, although it may be that instead of reaching a position where you 'possess' such attributes, you are required to gain a new personal perspective and understanding of influence in the world, rather than demonstrating it yourself. Much depends upon your ability to apply your talents and resources practically; potentially, your ideas and schemes can have a noticeable impact upon the world and your immediate environment, especially when you are working through an established structure and social system. This is because you feel more naturally in tune with existing organisations, preferring traditional approaches and attitudes as a reflection of 'stability and foundation'. You often resist accepting new trends or social changes, as you are inherently wary of them, preferring to follow your established path unless the impulse for change is naturally arising within yourself, and even then the likelihood is that you will attempt to resist and block its movement as a reaction to its unsettling effect. You will have a conservative nature and perception of life, respecting traditions and the consensus social attitudes, being suspicious of those who need to experiment and challenge accepted attitudes.

The socially subversive nature of Pluto is unlikely to be too evident, as Saturn will overlay it too much, although it can erupt in your inner and personal life, potentially stimulating a collapse in your 'secure foundations', forcing you to re-evaluate yourself and your life. Such a radical impact is unlikely, however, unless you are capable of undergoing the cathartic transformation that could occur, because Saturn will maintain your inner structure to prevent this happening.

You will be a private person, serious and secretive in nature, not openly revealing your thoughts and particularly your emotions, which you may try to avoid and keep tightly sealed away in a 'locked draw'. Emotions imply fluctuation and change to you, and this does not fit easily with your world view and perception of self, making you feel uncomfortable. A more healthy approach to emotions should be encouraged as it would prevent any energy repression on the emotional level, or else you may find that Pluto takes that route to make its presence felt.

In intimate relationships, you will be a firm, reliable partner, and you will prefer a traditional approach to marriage and mutual commitment, so you should choose wisely. You will not be overly demonstrative or emotional (on the surface), but you should avoid any tendency to fix the relationship in limiting and binding ties, allow it space to change and evolve. Remember that your partner is a unique individual with a potential to unfold, so allow the necessary freedom for them to do so, and encourage the process too. Security in a 'straightjacket' situation is a false situation, and inimical to growth and development, so despite your tendency in that direction, it is wiser to accept change and unpredictability so that energies can flow healthily.

Saturn–Pluto Sextile

You should have the ability to organise, control and focus your will-power effectively in order to achieve your ambitions. Similar to those with the conjunction, you can act as a 'magician' transmitting occult energies and influence through established structures; the purpose of such impulses will be varied, sometimes constructive, sometimes destructive or preservative in their initial impact and appearance. A Pluto impact via Saturn can seem to be very negative and destructive at first, as it can shatter the existing foundations, yet its purpose is rebirth and regeneration, breaking old outgrown limitations to create the space for the new direction to emerge through.

You may need to learn how to apply this energy in a practical way, probably through a self-initiated discipline and clear awareness of the way in which you wish to use it. Certainly, you will need to consider your aims carefully, planning and adjusting your approach according to strengths and weaknesses.

Success is important to you, materially and psychologically, and you will try very hard to become an achiever in whichever sphere of life you choose. Some degree of frustration is inevitable, but you tend to believe that with perseverance and a realistic self-appraisal you are capable of success – eventually. You believe that experience is the best teacher, and that a sign of intelligence is to make full use of that experience for the purposes of growth, and that involves learning and understanding life's lessons as soon as possible, to avoid unnecessary painful repetition. You can be intolerant of others who learn slowly, or who insist on repeating the same mistakes over and over again, thus spoiling their own lives. Taking responsibility for one's own life is important to you, and you understand the crucial role of choice in life, knowing that a life is determined by the nature of choices made, whether seemingly important or trivial in nature. Unwise choices invariably lead to more suffering for yourself and others, and could often be avoided if more thought and awareness were applied before decisions were taken.

A feeling of security is important to you, reflecting the known boundaries of Saturn, yet you are more alive to the necessity of change in life, and are less inclined to resist this than are those with the Saturn–Pluto conjunction. Emotionally, you accept the inner mutability and flow more naturally, and so do not create a problem of emotionally based repression erupting into an uncontrollable destructiveness in your relationships.

Saturn–Pluto Trine

As with the sexile aspect, this indicates that you will have a good organising ability, using your concentrated will-power to make the maximum use of your talents and resources, provided that you have clearly defined your purposes in the light of your real potential.

The concept of a manipulator of energies - or magician - is evident, and you will naturally use subtle energies to help achieve your will; this may be applied either consciously with deliberation, or as an unconscious psychological projection or emanation from you. This ability can be developed through forms of self-training, and you are likely to be attracted to occultism, astrology, magic, yoga and science, appropriate areas in which to investigate subtle energies through personal experience. You may have a sense of underlying purpose in your life, perceived as a fated path which is both unfolding naturally from within you, yet is a path that you feel you have to follow towards an unknown destination.

It can be that this meaningful path of purpose threading through your life has the effect of stimulating essential change and transformation in the lives of yourself and others, and is a 'calling' from the transpersonal dimension as reflected by Pluto.

You are capable of handling wisely any leadership or managerial responsibilities that you achieve, and you should be able to obtain the co-operation of others by your sensitivity to their feelings and openness to their ideas. Basically, you value people and have respect for others, and you use your powers of persuasion not to abuse the trust of others or take personal advantage, but to develop constructive harmony.

You accept the inevitability of change in life, especially in social spheres, and you may apply your talents to social transformation. You are less accepting of change in your intimate relationships, however, as you prefer things to remain in the same pattern once it has been satisfactorily established. You may feel inclined to use your 'subtle forces' to protect and restrict such a relationship, and whilst it may be quite protective in effect, you do have to remember the necessity for personal growth and development, and that an atmosphere of mutual freedom is preferable. If you choose your partner wisely, there is the potential for a relatively stable partnership to develop, where both can unfold their unique potentiality over many years.

Saturn–Pluto Square

With this aspect, it is likely that you will feel quite restricted by social and environmental constraints, and that the influence of the society in which you live will have considerable impact upon your life, often appearing to be a negative one.

Frustration appears to be inevitable, and you may feel that you are having to carry 'a burden for society', where you are involved in some way with a personal responsibility for some of society's troubles. This could be a form of work which takes you into problem areas, or even a sense of inner attunement to the sufferings of the world. There is a form of linking between your personal unfoldment and growth with the struggles of mass humanity, one which you may experience or interpret in a peculiarly masochistic manner, or use as an excuse for personal failings.

Some of this tendency could arise from earlier life and parental relationships and conditioning, possibly from environmental deprivation or lack of fulfilling and meaningful contact with your parents and family.This can lead to a pattern of personal disappointments and lack of essential trust in life and the world, leaving you emotionally marked and feeling insecure and uneasy with yourself, creating a lack of confidence in your own abilities and talents. You may feel 'hard done by', and feel envious of others who appear to be enjoying life and succeeding; there can be a 'chip on your shoulder' and a corrosive inner bitterness affecting your basic attitude.

When you do make extra efforts to make progress towards your aims, you often feel that you are being strangely hindered by events, people and circumstances which arise to frustrate, divert and block your attempts. Even though it may not appear so, this is likely to be the result in the outer world of inner projections, where through your own attitudes of defeatism and fear of success you trigger a reaction in the world to oppose you. You can create your own failure without consciously realising it.

You tend to be searching for status, power and the opportunity to influence people's lives, much in the same way that you feel your own life has been affected by nameless unknown others who make socially influential decisions. There is an element of wanting to dominate within you, possibly to 'get your own back' through blaming others for any problems that you have had.

To transform this oppressive pattern of limitation, you will need to radically alter your outlook on life and your self. The Pluto energy will help you to achieve this, and the first step is to draw back all the projections that you are overlaying on the world, and to recognise those that place the reason for failure 'out there'. You need to accept responsibility for your own life, decisions and choices, and begin to take control instead of being a frustrated, passive reactor.

Many have transcended difficult environmental barriers through assertiveness and effort of will, succeeding in breaking limitations and creating a life that satisfies them, and you need not be the exception to this possibility: the solution lies in your own psyche. Choose to change, observe the repetitive patterns of excuses and lack of commitment to succeed, and then override them through discipline and concentrated will. You are that 'mysterious barrier' opposing your own efforts; release the negativity that you cling to, and it will seem that a new world will open up for you, where you can begin to make progress, a world where more light can penetrate and illuminate the darkness. Remember, it is your own choice to remake your own life.

Saturn–Pluto Opposition

Like those with the square, you may feel that you have been mysteriously penalised by environmental deprivation, socially or parentally, real or imagined. There was never any 'silver spoon' for you, and you tend to hold a brooding resentment for those who have not had to face the same problem.

The opposition is often associated with the themes of oppression and violence, physical and psychological, and with the tendency to be a victim of such forms of human negativity on others. For whatever reason, you may feel yourself to be a victim of persecution, and this would colour your perception of people and the world, probably making you inwardly defensive and possibly outwardly aggressive towards others as a form of pre-emptive defence.

Your ease of self-expression and creativity is likely to be blocked, and you are always wary of revealing too much of yourself to others, in case they begin to take advantage of you, and in any case, you lack self-confidence and inner stability. Emotionally, you may be quite unstable, probably repressing much of your feeling life, because that is what has been damaged previously. This leads you to attempt to create a life of predictability and stability as a counterpoint to those feelings of emotional flux and vulnerability. Certainly you are quite resistant to change, especially within relationships as you rely on those few close ones in your life to give a sense of security, and because of this fear, you suppress inner movement or outer change until a crisis point is reached where a 'releasing explosion' is the only way for the blocked energy to move.

As with the square, you need to initiate a process of inner change, to transform the restrictive attitudes and self-image that act as a frustrating factor in your life. Somehow, you need to develop more personal confidence so that you can begin trusting more, and feel secure enough to come to terms with your feelings and emotions, to allow them to fertilise and water those inner barren lands. Through such an approach, Pluto can act to give you a new birth, to almost resurrect you from the dead and to allow you the opportunity to enjoy life much more fully and appreciatively. Your inner life is not fixed in unchangeable stone, as the prospect of transformation is everpresent in every life. Initially, it may be difficult to dissolve such long-established barriers, but it can be done, enabling a new you to flower and fulfil your hidden potential: this is the pot of gold which is waiting for you to claim it as your heritage.

URANUS–PLUTO ASPECTS

Uranus–Pluto Conjunction

The aspects of Uranus to Pluto tend to be socially and generationally orientated, and the qualities, tendencies and attitudes associated with them are those which give a distinct conditioning tone to society during the period of the aspect. The conjunction is quite rare, being made in the last century around 1848, a time of revolution in Europe, and occurring again in the period of 1963–68, a time of great civil unrest and social change in Europe and America.

The influence of these potent transpersonal planets is likely to be radical and far-reaching, the impact setting a direction for the following century to develop and integrate, and which requires a long period of time for society to assimilate the nature of the change which has occurred. In that sense, the influence is worldwide, and the period in which the close aspect of a conjunction is made should be carefully analysed to perceive the essential thrust of this directive energy and the emergent trends of society's development over the next hundred years.

With the cosmic periodic releasing of such powerful energies, the human reaction to them is varied and often polarised in response. These reveal the interface between the individual life and the collective life of a society. It is as though from a multiplicity of sources a new alluring voice is rising, which is revealing a new approach to life for society to absorb. Certain individuals respond enthusiastically to this new siren call, embracing 'the new way', and begin to group together as like-minded collaborators to become an influential minority within their own society. They then reflect the new ideas, impregnate society with them and act as transmitters of change. Broader social reaction to 'the new way' is often slow, apart from the inevitable reaction against the new trend, and often society attempts to use the power of its established structures to resist what appears to be a threatening impulse.

The influence of the conjunction is to initiate a new phase of social change, and during the 1963–68 aspect, it was that of a revolutionary spirit in the air, extolling the virtues of individual rights and freedom, stimulating the need for the transformation of the existing social establishment and the breakdown of outdated and limiting social and national attitudes and ingrained patterns of thinking.

For those who were (and still are) attuned and receptive to this visionary energy, there is a personal feeling of involvement in a vast process of evolutionary development occurring on earth, a feeling that their individual life is intimately linked with a vast plan slowly unfolding into manifestation, and that their lives are guided by some greater consciousness; participants in a planetary drama. As a worldwide group joined together by shared response, they collectively form a channel for the new social approach to be mediated into human life and consciousness. Some reflect this in a more unconscious manner, some seek to manifest the overshadowing energy via conscious meditation or occult rituals, etc.

What is of importance to this group is a respect for life, in all of its forms, ranging from human life to that of animals and plants, all of the many appearances of nature and the abundant creativity of Earth. Life is viewed as essentially 'holy', to be cherished, respected, enjoyed and protected. It is a basic attitude to life that wants the highest quality of life for everyone founded upon a balanced and careful relationship with the environment and the natural world, where human society moves from being a dangerous exploiter of nature's gifts to live in a more natural harmony. Individually, there is the need to develop as a unique person, free to live and express ourselves in our own right as far as possible, based on peaceful co-operative coexistence, to learn how to unfold innate potentiality provided it does not infringe on the rights of others.

Viewing the world situation some twenty years after the close conjunction, the attitudes released into the world at this time are still serving as a needed social direction, and many pressure groups have been formed to further the progress of such causes. The succeeding century needs to see more development for the benefit of mankind.

Uranus–Pluto Sextile

The sextile aspect occurred in the midst of the Second World War, and it could be considered that the nature of the energy released during 1942–46 was a positive boost to the Allied forces at the time, as it stimulated their cohesiveness and commitment to fighting against the oppressive Nazi regime.

If actually applied in the world, the tendencies associated with the sextile of Uranus–Pluto would help bring about social improvement and clarity within government and publicly representative bodies. It invokes a natural voice of the people to speak out against social injustice and hypocrisy, to resist dictatorial abuse of power and influence emanating from central government, and to expose corruption in high places wherever it occurs. It embodies the dichotomy between the individual and the state, wherein the state should reflect the democratic will of the people, and be the elected servant of the people, and yet in real life becomes an independent entity, dominated by power-blocks and influential political parties, which perceives itself as being superior to the people and often ignores their wishes. The political élite is often quite dismissive of the general public, believing that it has the machinery and power to manipulate the social consciousness as it wills, and it invariably wishes that democracy – or whatever passes for it – did not exist to get in its way.

Unfortunately, the analysis of public apathy and the élite's ability to manipulate social attitudes is often correct, and serves as a reactionary barrier to social progress. However, one tendency of this aspect is to expect and insist upon a high quality of governmental leadership, whereby those in positions of authority and social influence should express the highest ideals, morals and values of the society they represent; if not, they should be replaced. A shift in this direction, assuming such quality people made themselves available, could stimulate a major change in society; it is a prerequisite for the new vision to appear in the future. Preserving and expanding the nature and depth of freedom in the world is an ongoing struggle, in the West as in the East, as there are many who wish to see it destroyed for self-centred reasons.

Of interest during these war years, was the rapid development of the Manhattan Project, and the birth of the atomic bomb, where the sudden 'lightning flash' quality of Uranus is demonstrated by the scientific intuitions and insights to create the technology and in the physical demonstration of its effect. Pluto displays its negative social face in this aspect, holding a sword of Damocles over the world, confronting us with a choice of two forms of transformation, negative and positive, collective destruction or collective unifying change. The way forward obviously depends upon public activism or apathy and the quality of social leadership and the nature of the conditioning attitude, separatist or unitive; and the circle turns to confront us with those tendencies associated with the sextile aspect, which collectively we are still facing.

Uranus–Pluto Trine

The trine aspect occurred during the 1920s, and stimulated an impulse towards international change, an urge to reform existing social and political structures. The acknowledgement of the need for this is displayed in the economic instability and collapse in America and Germany, the British depression and the creation of the new Communist regime in Russia. In addition, new political approaches emerged as Fascism, National Socialism, Communism – all founded on 'new' ideals and ideologies, and yet all often demonstrating an outlook liable to cause international conflict, despite domestic social improvements in individual countries.

Change was in the air; many were responding to its heady effect, trying to take advantage of the energies recently released to them, and there is a feeling of a searching and experimentation during a time of crisis and transition, when little seemed clear and definite, and most seemed part of an international melting pot, the results of which could define the direction of the future.

There was a new willingness to break free of the past, an openness to all new ideas and developments. Some welcomed this with excitement, but as cultural and social structures began to dissolve or lose their influence, some found the changes disturbing, feeling the sands beneath their feet shifting too rapidly for them to feel secure. Those under the trine's influence felt that the tide of history was moving with them, and that no obstacle could stand in their way for long. The traditional ways were considered outdated and restrictive; they were looking for something new in which they could discover some form of personal meaning, and with emotional enthusiasm they flocked to support the newly emergent political philosophies which appeared to embody the new world they felt was imminent.

The Uranus–Pluto trine acted as a channel for energies to stimulate national characteristics, and to dissolve the power of tradition and the past. It shook the world, and initially – as we are now able to observe with the benefit of hindsight – it had a destructive impact, yet one which was necessary in order to clear the ground for the more constructive influence to emerge. It gave a boost to scientific and intellectual development in the West, yet stimulated a relatively immature emotional level in society, which found early security by becoming part of mass emotional support for those charismatic demagogues who rose to the forefront of the political arena. In some ways, the effects of the trine are the direct reverse to those of the previous opposition aspect which occurred at the turn of the century, 1900–1903, almost as if the 'turning of the screw' created even more social confusion and conflict within the period of the World Wars. Certainly the changes occurring within this century have been profound and extensive, a rapidly moving series of crises developing in every aspect of life, leading towards some epochal crescendo.

Uranus–Pluto Square

The influence of the square aspect was to stimulate 'destructive' social change across international borders, to intensify all those latent nationalistic characteristics that had been coming to the surface of the national group minds, until the only way both to express and release the underlying tensions was through world conflict.

The close square applied from 1931 to 1934, and the phase was of rapid metamorphosis in crucial countries like Germany and Italy. These were two clear examples of the impact of the Uranian-Plutonian energy, where nationalistic tendencies and élitist attitudes were elevated into a sense of social direction, manipulated by dictatorial groupings in an attempt both to seize power and to benefit the state by introducing new political concepts. The power complex and need to dominate of the unregenerated Pluto energy is displayed in the need to expand their control and influence into other less powerful nations, through ruthlessly expressed violence and force.

The general world economic instability helped to create the space for radical and revolutionary political agitators to come into positions of power, feeding off the exploited energy of will (Pluto) to build an apparently attractive new society. In many cases, this basic urge to create new social structures was genuinely held by those whose motives and ideals were socially beneficial; however, they were to lose their positions of responsibility to those whose intentions were more mixed, and who were being swept along by their receptiveness to the powerful energies pouring into the world, which served to over-stimulate aspects of their unintegrated personalities.

The collective group responding to the fascist and Nazi ideals were generating and reflecting the possessing energy, especially through the group mind and seen in those emotionally manipulative and evocative mass public rallies, which were similar in effect to certain types of magical rituals. There were two main ways in which people reacted to the social change occurring; one was to collaborate with it, being excited and thrilled by being a positive participant in a national resurrection, irrespective of some of the hidden darker aspects. The other way was to be apathetic and passive, allowing it to go on all around them, feeling insecure and unable to have any influence even if they disagreed with the dominating group.

What became paramount in this square was the stimulation of the unconscious national mind and emotions by Pluto, which overrode the more intellectually idealistic mind quality of Uranus. All those repressed tendencies rose into physical view, those attitudes of superiority, of national frustration, of harsh, sadistic dismissal of other 'inferior races'. Together with the power of violent aggression, they became integrated into the expression of the new society, and freedom was ignored by the oppressor. The dark face of incorrectly applied Pluto energy was ready to be unleashed onto the world.

Uranus–Pluto Opposition

At the time of the opposition, in 1900–1903, the traditional social establishment and class structure in the West was at its peak, and feeling that it was culturally advanced and essentially invulnerable to erosion from 'subversives'. This is not to imply that no change was happening, but that the ruling élite considered itself secure at that time. The monarchies appeared still to be strong in certain nations, social attitudes and divisions were clearly defined, and exploitation of the colonies held the key to economic expansion at little cost. The star of the British Empire was at its zenith and many thought that (relatively) all was well with the world.

The shadow of the opposition began to lengthen, disturbing the calm and the status quo, and suspicions began to deepen regarding the early stirrings of new developments in new thinking, culturally, politically and socially. Whilst these would still take several years to burst into open public view, this was their gestation period, prior to the crises of World War, the Russian Revolution, and economic collapse.

The rumblings of the underground reshaping of the world began to be heard by some on the surface, who felt as if they were sitting on the peak of a volcano previously thought to be extinct. Occultism began to be more attractive to many in the West, reflecting the need for inner transmutation experienced by people, and several major occult personalities who were to emerge into greater attention during the early 1920s (period of the trine), such as Alice Bailey, Steiner and Gurdjieff, were undergoing their earlier phases of experience, training and initiation at this time. Of interest is the release in April 1904 of the 'Book of the Law' through Aleister Crowley in the Cairo workings, where the 'Word of the New Aeon' was transmitted into the world consciousness. It is as if this occult announcement and the Uranus–Pluto opposition were both sounding the death-knell of the old order and the birth of the new.

The changes triggered at this time, the commencement of a new century, and the last in this millennium, are still reverberating today, many of them still unresolved or transferred to different exponents of national conflicts. There is still the need for more people capable of thinking for themselves, for people to be less dependent upon others to make decisions for them, to reduce the power of individual authority figures and élites, and to share power and responsibility for society amongst its members.

The influence of the Uranian ideals was opposed by the need for an emotionally biased sense of security represented by the familiar and traditional ways; the clash between them bringing world disruption. The influence of Pluto was initially used to give support to the old ways, but is correctly received as a means of subverting the establishment, so that the new can be born, a process that we are still experiencing.

NEPTUNE–PLUTO ASPECTS

Neptune–Pluto Sextile

During this century, there is only one major aspect made between Neptune and Pluto – the sextile – and it is interesting to note that it commenced in the midst of the Second World War during 1942. The influence of this relationship would be expected to have global and generational effects, and like all of the transpersonal planetary energies, would be a directive force stimulating the unfoldment of the evolutionary process within time and space.

Neptune will attract an almost mystical exploratory search from those responsive to it, and since the sextile commenced, science has reacted in two distinct and complementary directions: effort has been poured into developing space travel and satellite technology, exploring the vast outer universe through radio-telescopes, etc.; and the complementary exploration of inner space, investigating and probing the building blocks of matter, and quantum physics has risen to the forefront of scientific enquiry.

The attempts to understand the nature of the universe, its composition and size, the possible creation of the universe and the 'big bang theory' reflect the traditional Western way of looking externally. What has paralleled this tendency has been the birth of an opposite movement amongst people, that of self-exploration, the inner mystical way. This is through the 'New Age' movement, humanistic/Jungian psychology, occult techniques and the rebirth of magical attitudes towards life. It also involves the grafting onto the Western tree of many of the attitudes and much of the knowledge of Eastern philosophies and religions, a merging of the two hemispheres, a potential unification of belief structures reflecting the scientific movement towards a more mystically orientated quantum physics.

As the outer universe becomes vaster, and the inner universe becomes a mysterious vastness of space, the only point in which the outer and the inner can become reconciled is in the human being. At a time when the immense destructive power of splitting the atom can be used to commit racial suicide or genocide, the old Mystery School injunction of the ancients is the key to the future: 'Man, Know Thyself'.

The generations born after this aspect commenced, together with those spiritual aspirants/initiates already living who respond to the higher vibrations of the transpersonal planets and thus intuit and respond to its influence, are aware of the basic tendencies emanating from it. They are life-enhancing, the need to protect the world's environment from senseless devastation, the need to extend individual rights and freedoms, to unfold international co-operation and to move beyond an embracing consumer materialist dominance in the West. The recognition that potentially a higher quality of life can be had in the world for the majority of people through a redirection of resources (if the will is there) can lead to radical change.

The energies of transformation are present, much depends upon our use of them, individually and collectively, for negative or positive results. The challenge of free will is the nature of choice and decision, which determine, in the present, the nature of the future.

RETROGRADE PLUTO

Retrograde Pluto tends to reflect the common human difficulty in creatively and positively working with the Pluto energy. It is a phase in which the conscious attention should be turning within, as a preparatory action prior to experiencing a deeper degree of personal integration. As has been previously noted, the natal house position represents the associations within life that should be highlighted for radical rebirth.

For most of humanity this highly refined, powerful energy will be felt primarily in an unconscious way, triggering an automatic response that often leads to negative results due to an inability to accept this energy and use it in a positive way.

The retrograde position indicates the potential of a power of regeneration within the personal/collective unconscious, whereas the direct motion indicates the need to act from this regenerated aspect of self into constructive socially orientated directions.

The essence of the problem confronting humanity and the individual is how to absorb and integrate the higher Pluto energy in a harmonious manner. For most people, it is virtually impossible at this time; for the minority who are forward orientated, it is their responsibility to function as conscious channels of response and action, and they should be willing to enter the sacrificial and transformative path for the benefit of others.

For any who are especially responsive to the Pluto energy, and in particular those in whose charts the motion is retrograde, there will be an inner sensitivity towards the planetary life and the pain and struggle of humanity. This is an empathic awareness, perhaps dimly formulated but nevertheless present, and is associated with the soul level of unity. It can be difficult to deal with, and the pressure of registering an impact from the world mind and emotions can often be extremely disturbing. This faculty is one which will become more prominent within humanity as time passes, and indicates a development in the level of consciousness. It stimulates the inner urge to 'change the world', to put an end to unnecessary suffering which primarily arises from incorrect states of self-identification.

The retrograde natal Pluto individual has the main task of healing himself, bringing about a personal rebirth, whereas the direct natal Pluto person should be more concerned with the application of the Pluto energy towards society. With transit motion, it indicates phases of 'in-breath and out-breath', times when reorientation may be required prior to further external activity or for inner adjustments or evaluation to be more productive on the out-breath stage.

EXALTED PLUTO IN LEO

Traditionally, Pluto is exalted in Leo and the 5th house, and deals with the concept of concentrated power being released by the directive will of the self-aware individual. Within the human body, Pluto is the progenitor of the capacity for physical and psychological regeneration, and the creative power of the 'seed'. To achieve this function, Pluto acts in the role as ruler of Scorpio, which is associated with the sexual organs.

Regeneration and seed creativity, within all the human levels of physical, emotional, mental and spiritual, is the destined purpose of this power. It involves renewing life, forming new life in order to replace those structures – individual and social – that are no longer capable of enduring a further regenerative process.

There is an association with the concept of a 'seed of spirit' which is seeking its release from unknown depths of the human nature. This is often linked with the Eastern belief in energy centres connected to the body called the chakra system, which sequentially open up and become activated as spiritual understanding expands. The most common delineation of this system has seven major chakras to be awakened, from the root of the spine, via the sexual centre, solar plexus, heart, throat, ajna/forehead, to the crown of the head. Activating these centres by self-exploration, meditation, ritual, etc., can be seen to raise this seed from the lowest chakra eventually to the crown. Each step towards stimulating each centre into action has corresponding effects within consciousness and sensitivity to life, and instigates a development in the essential integration and wholeness of the seeker. The raising of the kundalini fire upwards through the spinal column is the effect of this seed, and corresponds to the increasing awareness that 'God is a consuming fire'.

The ability of humanity to discover the secret of the power hidden within nature and its atomic structure, at the time when Pluto was in the sign of Leo, is paralleled by this hidden 'seed' within the individual. The opening of the seed and the energy released can be felt much as an 'inner atomic explosion', and reflects the fact that the outer is a mirror image of the inner reality. It is indisputable that the splitting of the atom, and the use to which this scientific knowledge has been put, has created a transition period of immense difficulty for humanity. We have the power of world destruction at our fingertips, yet the ability for regenerating or creating a new world is not really known to us yet; certainly, it never will become common knowledge until the time comes when it is evident that we will not use the destructive power. It appears that man initially responds to new higher energies in a negative way, before the more positive dimension becomes clear. Through Leo and the 5th house, the way forward is by resolving the basic dualistic polarities within mind and body, and that achievement would inaugurate a new phase of real creativity for the individual and society.

Natal Chart Examples

As two examples of the influence of an emphasised Pluto energy within the natal chart, I have chosen the data related to Margaret

Thatcher and Karl Marx. Perhaps an odd coupling, but their charts do indicate the underlying activities of Pluto, having several major aspects made to Pluto allied to the life-time themes associated with the house position of Pluto. It is suggested that in reading the comments below you refer to the charts themselves and to the aspect and house analyses given earlier.

Margaret Thatcher

In Margaret Thatcher's chart, Pluto is in the 8th house, there is a Scorpio Ascendant, and there are six major aspects to Pluto: Sun square, Mars square, Jupiter opposition, Saturn trine, Uranus trine and Ascendant trine. So she is Libra Sun with a very dominant Pluto emphasis.

It seems to me that evaluating her in terms solely of this Pluto influence on her life and political attitudes and style is quite apt and interesting; certainly this seems to reflect the perceptions of her held by her antagonists.

The difficulties of a Libran trying to centre the swinging scales are not aided by the subversion of the Scorpio Ascendant, and these tensions will amplify those obsessive tendencies in her nature. In an attempt to handle these inner tensions, she fixes her mind into an unmovable pattern – 'the lady is not for turning' – and tries to carve in stone her unbreakable, fixed attitudes. Re-evaluation and change of course are not amongst the options she allows herself – at least in public!

Her need to be in control, authoritative and dominant are emanating from the Scorpio/Pluto energy, and so is the image of her as a form of warrior woman, 'the Iron Lady'; this is reminiscent of the esoteric keynote associated with Scorpio, 'Warrior I am, and from the battle I emerge triumphant!'

As she says, she is a 'conviction politician', certain of her own path and the rightness of her attitudes and beliefs; for her 'there is no alternative'. She prefers to remain with the obsessive side of Plutonian energy rather than align with its transformative nature. A study of the aspect and house analyses reveals the personal inner alternatives that she has had (it is doubtful whether she could change now), and the inner conflicts that she has experienced, even the choices that it appears that she has made during her life.

Karl Marx

Karl Marx is a world-famous political philosopher, renowned for his economic, social and political theories and ideology, the foundation for the development of Communist and socialist thinking which has been so prevalent during this century.

Marx has five major Pluto aspects in his natal chart: Venus sextile, Mars trine, Saturn conjunction, Uranus square and Neptune square; and his natal Pluto is in the 2nd house (using Equal Houses – 1st house using the Placidean system).

In his personal life, Marx was dependent upon his wife, especially for economic support for the family, as she was a member of the wealthy Engels family, and it is quite likely that he suffered certain psychosomatic illnesses created by emotional repression stimulated by his obsession with the development of his politico-economic theories and preoccupation with the intellectual level of activity. He wrote his classic *Das Kapital* whilst living in England, and in many ways it was a response to the English class society at the time.

It is interesting to consider that his natal Pluto was in the house of materialism and resources, and that his own personal struggle for economic survival and material possessions is part of his own 'obstacle' (2nd house) which needed resolving. Essentially, much of his private struggle and obsession was absorbed within his theories and elevated to the universal level – that of his interpretation of man and society. This espoused a predominantly materialistic perception of humanity, regarding man as subservient to the greater whole, the state. Marx attempted to convey the concept of stewardship of resources for the benefit of others, and to reach a new personal understanding of materialism at its most positive – true to his 2nd house Pluto.

The Mars–Pluto trine appears to be quite apt, and the Saturn conjunction notes the emotional repression that began to develop in his life as his ideas began to obsess him more, and affected his relationship with his wife, who none the less stood by him and the family and continued to support his efforts, which reflects the implication that the partnership was fated to occur. The Uranus–Pluto square is mainly considered in terms of this century, but it was through a Marxist ideology that a dictator like Stalin was able to express the energy of that square. The square with Neptune associates the individual with the destiny of the collective, and influences the awareness of the need to transform unsuitable existing structures and patterns of thought into something new to embody future directions. Marx made this attempt, although he limited himself within the confines of his own personal preoccupations and challenges, and this affected his political philosophy to physical and materialistic concerns and analyses of the nature of collective man. The influence of his efforts has spread across time and national barriers, being adopted, modified and distorted by those who accept his premises (or those upon whom they are imposed). From a humanistic standpoint it is too limiting to see man as primarily an economic creature; but again, the Pluto emphasis is revealing of the hidden inner impulses at work, those inner conflicts in an individual which in this case led to the creation of a world political philosophy influencing the history and destiny of man.

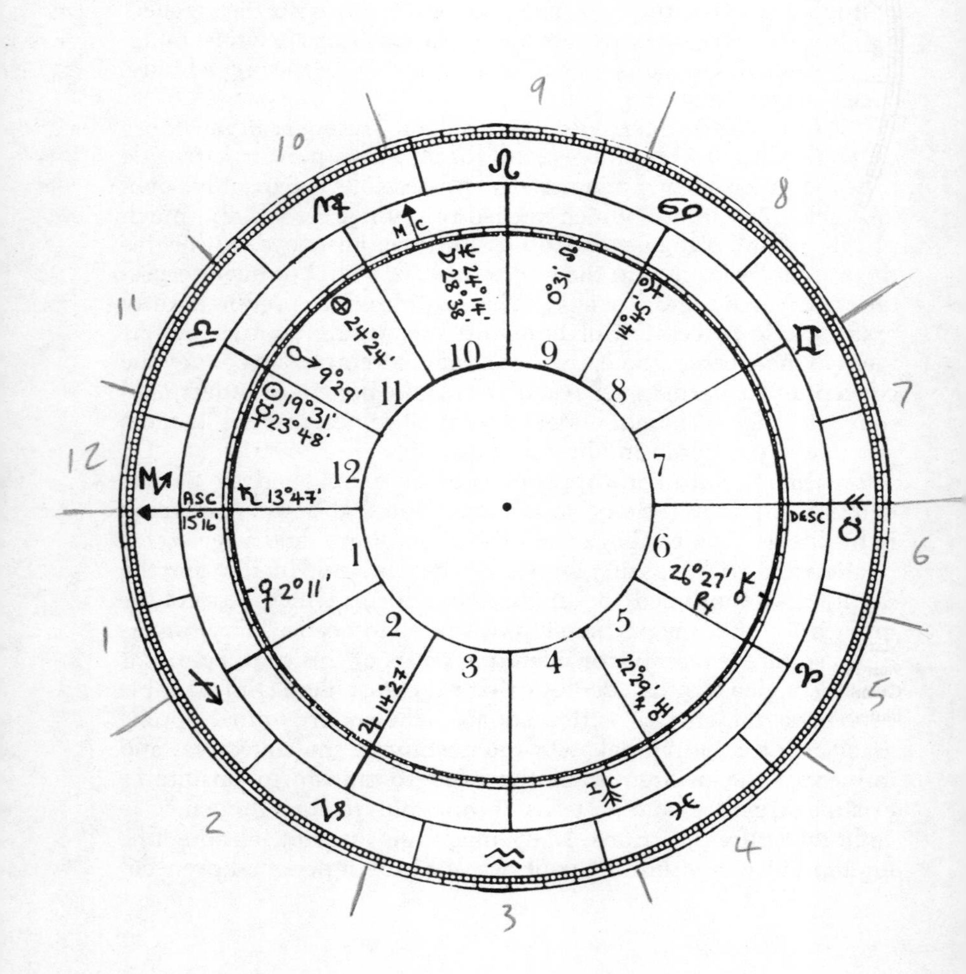

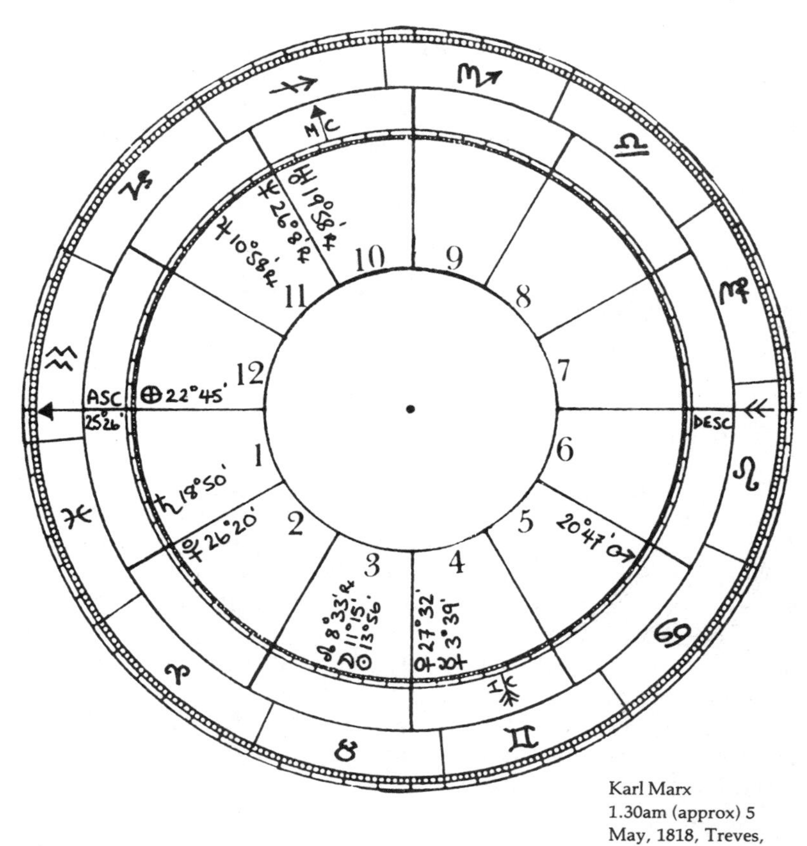

Karl Marx
1.30am (approx) 5 May, 1818, Treves, Prussia
Pluto Sextile Venus
Trine Mars
Conjunct Saturn
Square Uranus
Square Neptune
Natal Pluto 2nd House

Margaret Thatcher
9am 13.10.1925
Grantham, England
Pluto Square Sun
Square Mars
Opposition Jupiter
Trine Saturn
Trine Uranus
Trine Ascendant
Natal Pluto 8th House

CHAPTER 5

Pluto in the Natal House

THE NATAL HOUSE POSITION OF PLUTO indicates both the sphere of life in which a personal, crystallised challenge of considerable difficulty is found, and also where the individual can make a valuable contribution to society. This can take two distinct forms. The first is where a socially beneficial effect only occurs as a result of a successful inner struggle with the personal difficulty; the second is where, in the process of the inner struggle, as a result of the pressure of conflict, some by-product or talent emerges from within which is socially beneficial. In this case, the actual problem does not even need to be solved, and in fact could fail to be for the remainder of the life. Both involve a rebirth in that area of life, one as a clear transformation, one as part of an attempt to change, but essentially both have a positive result.

Depending upon the degree of self-understanding, it should be quite obvious to a person which areas of life need adjusting in order to gain an improved quality of experience. If it is an area in which certain shadow characteristics fall, then it is possible that a state of 'blindness' may be psychologically imposed, and they fail to register that perhaps their attitude or form of social expression is the source of most of their problems in life. If the natal house position of Pluto is known, then it can be a key to unlock many inner doors, because its influence will certainly be potent, and should be explored to discover what the 'obstacle' reveals and suggests as to where consciously directed energy should be focused in order to liberate this unexpressed psychic energy.

For the individual, the experience of this is invariably hard. Often it seems to be an insurmountable problem, and like Pluto's transits, it seems to be lasting for ever, and yet it cannot be shaken from the conscious mind, becoming an obsession. It is in fact an opportunity that is slowly building up, even though from a disturbed standpoint this rarely seems the case. It is like an old shell of past or still existing attitudes which are outmoded, yet still have great power locked into them, and slowly this 'shell' begins to inflate, demanding that the conscious self confronts it and deals with it.

Somehow, this 'shell' needs to be punctured, releasing its imprisoned, frustrated energy so that new forms of expression can be developed on the impetus of the liberated vitality. This may require a leap of faith in a direction that the individual intuits is the right one to move towards, without having any real, objective proof that it is a wise action to take. The life may be turned upside down, creating a crisis or turning point for a decisive break with the past to be made. It may be that the individual just stops what they have been doing, stopping a frenetic lifestyle of work and socialising to review exactly what they are doing with their lives, and considering whether it fulfils them.

To gain a sense or feeling of the reality of Pluto, try to tune into that area of life associated with your natal Pluto, and observe how it seems to have an influence that also permeates the rest of your life, a deep, personally meaningful part of your existence that is also felt as a vulnerability. Review your life in terms of these associations, and see if your experiences and choices which are directly linked with these associations seem to have a noticeable relevance and importance to your life in terms of success and enjoyment (fate). Or perhaps they are linked to that 'problem area' which you struggle to resolve in some way, or realise that you need to make changes within? Wherever Pluto resides in the natal chart, or where there is a strong Scorpio bias, you are likely to discover a powerful reservoir of energy which needs careful conscious handling for success; it can turn to destroy your life or help to remake it.

Whatever the results of this confrontation, the key to resolving the problem of the 'battleground' is in the natal house position of Pluto. It may be wise to remember that to fulfil the underlying purpose of Pluto, individual transformation also becomes a contribution to a broader progressive social awakening. It is one way in which the individual becomes more aware of his inner relationship with the collective mentality of his society.

Natal Pluto in the 1st House

The 1st house is the sphere of personal identity, and the placing of Pluto in this natal house indicates that an area of difficulty and inner conflict will be centred in the living experience of the separate self.

Pluto will attempt to lead you towards transformation through your sense of self-identity. Your earlier upbringing and home life may have been difficult, possibly as a result of a broken home, or parental conflicts and financial worries which led to a conscious focus and struggle to fulfil basic material needs. Certainly, you will feel as though you had a hard, testing and challenging early life, one which has had a considerable impact upon the development of your personality, outlook on life and sense of self-worth.

As Pluto undermines efforts if they are not fully suitable for its hidden purpose and goal, you may find that through people and situations the external environment is liable to thwart many of your attempts to express your own personal nature and aims. Frustrated and probably restricted in such ways, you are likely to have a deep feeling of insecurity, hiding behind a defensive and reserved attitude. You will prefer to remain a social loner, and others will find it hard to penetrate behind the surface mask and control in order to get to know you better; often, you prefer to keep people at arm's length.

You like to feel that you are controlling your own life, and you can achieve this to some degree by your natural ability to be independent and by applying personal initiative and will-power towards attaining your self-created ambitions. As you often find it difficult to conform to societal ways and traditions of conduct and life-directions, this can create many problems for your individualist nature.

Your personality can be experienced by others as being forceful and even domineering, almost obsessive in its focus on the attainment of your purpose. This can create problems in your close relationships, marriage and your work, as all can be considered of secondary importance to achieving your objectives.

You may find yourself tempted to play games with people which involve elements of personal dominance, confrontation and exploitation of personal power, partly expressing your need for self-assertion and to establish your sense of identity. These 'games' can include emotional and mental manipulation, and tendencies in such a direction should be wisely curbed.

Your intimate relationships are likely to be extremely intense, characterised by a feeling of fate or destiny about them, and apparently arising without either partner obviously controlling their development and progress. They can be a main source of the transformative energy, providing you are able to create an equality in the relationship, and listen to your partner without having to dominate and control in order to feel secure.

You will need to become regenerated through a deeper understanding of your own nature, and to gain insight into the inner turmoil beneath the cool surface, which can release that unused energy in positive creative ways. You can possess a powerful will and ability to concentrate, and this should be used for the benefit of others through a dedication to higher social ideals. This will also serve to reintegrate your sense of personal identity into a regenerated form, thus fulfilling the intention of Pluto.

Natal Pluto in the 2nd House

This house is concerned with the appropriate use of resources, especially material possessions, and the Pluto influence will emphasise an inner compulsion and need within you to feel a sense of security through surrounding yourself with tangible physical signs of your success.

The dominating obsession will be to acquire money and material possessions, which you believe will give a feeling of security and personal power and control. This drive can create considerable inner friction, as all energies and thoughts are directed towards achieving your material goals. Obviously, this can have a direct impact upon your relationships with others, including perhaps a lack of time and interest for home and family except as 'possessions', and a tendency to become too selfish and greedy can lead to problems with the law, taxes, speculation or inheritances. If you are the main provider for a family, you may tend to exploit your position of power over them, especially through forms of financial domination instead of sharing through love.

What is needed is for you to transform this compulsion related to a need for security through money and materialism, of owning and controlling, into new, more inclusive values, and to discover positive personal meaning within yourself which is not dependent upon physical possessions. Basically, you need to release this obsessive energy, so that you become free of this 'devil of materialism', and to cleanse your desires and motives, so that you can embrace the concept of stewardship of resources which can be used and shared to benefit others too. If you allow the compulsion to direct your choices and decisions in life, then inevitably you will find that it is leading towards your downfall, and future alienation from others can lead potentially to financial problems. This is because Pluto wants you to change in this sphere of life, to help you find a new personal understanding of the materialist impulse, and would eventually subvert all your efforts to build a sense of security in that direction if you are not attempting to change your attitudes. In some cases, the reaction to this tendency can be reversed and a form of inverted materialism may be expressed in a miserly attitude, where a fear of spending restricts the enjoyment of life, which is essentially as unbalanced as a tendency towards compulsive spending and conspicuous affluence. The real quality of a person is never measured by the size of his bank balance, or by a large house, new car, etc.; real quality is expressed in how the life is lived. Is it lived with social awareness and concern for the well-being of all, as an expression of a tolerant understanding and loving spirit? That is the real guide. Certainly, there is no real security in material possessions; the drive towards that is but one of the many illusions fostered by the contemporary consumer society.

Natal Pluto in the 3rd House

In this position of natal Pluto, the emphasis lies upon communication and the expressing of self and ideas, especially through words, either spoken or written.

This need to communicate can seem to be almost compulsive, and is both an effort to reach out and contact others, and a need to release an overactive inner energy. Whilst this energy can also be transmitted via the hands, often in healing, you are most likely to use it through speech, as there is a natural affinity and talent with words, and the likelihood is that you can develop into an effective, powerful speaker.

The energy is basically linked to the mental level, and you will have a sharp and penetrating mind, with your ideas on life carefully thought out, organised, and the ability to express your opinions and beliefs strongly to others. You can develop your own original ideas, and you will be attracted towards communicating them to others, so that they can help to spread them through society. This clear expression of ideas can be a way for you to gain influence and control over people, as your ability to persuade is considerable. You may have to be wary of any tendencies developing that lead you to abuse this talent, by taking advantage of others and dominating them.

Despite your clarity of expression, you will have to realise that in itself, this does not mean that the content of your ideas is invariably right. Anyone who can communicate effectively to others is liable to fall into this trap, and become ego-inflated, seeing others as inferior, treating them with a patronising attitude, and believing that what they themselves think and say is naturally correct. That illusion is a dangerous one, for yourself and others, and allows no space for real communication to occur.

Another tendency is to become fixed in your beliefs and opinions, so that there can be no compromise and change occurring over time as a natural result of greater life experience and deeper thought. Your way of perceiving life and interpreting meaning is your own, and may not be suitable for others, so any dogmatic approach is always restrictive and futile.

Pluto is attempting to lead you to realise that what you think and communicate to others will have consequences, great or small, depending upon your degree of social influence. This involves responsibility for what you transmit into the world, so be very aware of your motivations and the quality of content, because it will have its inevitable effect.

In your relationships, you will have to avoid a tendency to scheme and manipulate, and you will need to learn how to listen more carefully to your partner, and not just see them as a foil to your own wit and cleverness.

You are likely to analyse and over-intellectualise your relationship, often maintaining a certain distance from your emotions, as you feel uncomfortable with them, and feelings are much more difficult to express fluently in words. Sometimes your words act as a smokescreen for you to hide behind; blow away this smokescreen and there may be less of real substance there than may initially appear to be the case. Your words may glitter but be hollow. Eventually you experience a loss of substance and meaning in life, or others begin to see you as essentially shallow, without any real contribution to make. However, if you can use it creatively and positively, with real awareness for others, you can greatly benefit from this energy.

NATAL PLUTO IN THE 4TH HOUSE

This implies a compulsive need to feel physically and emotionally secure, and is likely to involve a tendency to retreat back into your physical home and internally within your feeling nature, as an attempt to evade any 'threats' that you feel are confronting you in the external world or whenever you feel unsure and insecure about life.

Essentially, you try to build your own personal 'castle', wherein you become lord and master as you hope to have total control over your immediate environment. The need to create your own private kingdom, may stem from your early life, where disruption and a lack of physical and emotional security may have existed, through perhaps the loss of a parent, or by family power struggles which affected you.

In your adult life, you will expend much energy on your 'castle' and family, and they will hold intense meaning and importance for you, representing an emotional and physical space into which you can retreat and relax, a controlled security. However, your need to maintain this control and stability can lead you to develop a dominating attitude, where your will and stubbornness in gaining your own way can lead to family friction. You may tend to 'imprison' others, through personal domination, as you build a protective but restrictive barrier between your 'castle' and the world; certainly you will be very resistant towards anything new entering the home life which might bring in disruptive elements, ideas, people, etc. You are likely to find it difficult to be aware of this demarcation line that you are drawing for others, of the way you restrict how they are allowed to experience the world, and of the limits to their personal freedom that you tend to insist upon. You manage the home environment in a way that makes others dependent upon you, and subservient to your demands. You need a partner who basically supports your emphasis on 'home as a castle', and who does not contradict your needs and values, but acts as a complement to them and is capable of maintaining an open contact for you and the family with the outer world.

To some degree, everyone expresses this tendency in home and family life, but with this Pluto placement, the likelihood of it being quite compulsive and obsessive is greatly emphasised, to the point where it could create problems for yourself and others. It is likely that in several ways your adult life at home could become quite disruptive and you could experience upheavals as a direct consequence of your attempts to satisfy your needs for security, particularly if imposed upon your family.

You are likely to be attracted towards exploring beneath the surface of things, with possibly considerable insight into the emotional depths of others through a natural attunement to the unconscious mind. Such a link will work both ways though, and Pluto will try to create conditions that transform your needs for physical/emotional security in a tangible form, towards greater self-understanding which can give you an inner sense of security not dependent upon outer supports. You should be striving to find an inner centre of peace and fulfilment, as ultimately this is more lasting than one based in the outer world.

Natal Pluto in the 5th House

You are likely to express the compulsion to feel important, to be in the public eye, and to be a known, recognised character. In short, you gain a strong feeling of self from the acknowledgement of others.

In many ways, this emerges as a compensatory factor for an inner sense of insecurity and personal inadequacy, a lack of self-confidence and understanding. You believe that if you are capable of projecting out into the world an image of yourself which is recognised by others, then somehow you become more important than you truly feel inside. Public recognition is a heady brew.

As this need to be important can be frustrated, and circumstances can conspire to divest it of its glamour by showing you the more negative aspects of public fame, you will need to undergo a thorough re-evaluation of this compulsion to be a 'somebody'. This may involve a process of self-examination, a coming to terms with your own nature and capabilities. Above all else, it may be advisable for you to achieve something of actual value which others can recognise as an expression of a personal skill or talent. This is preferable to the frustration of desiring to be a name and a face in the public eye, and yet being unable to 'deserve' such fame in any way.

You will have a certain creative talent, possibly an artistic one, and if you succeed in directing this energy towards practical expression, then you may begin to explore undiscovered areas and 'make your name' as a pioneer.

You will be attracted towards love affairs and children, as part of your need to enjoy the pleasures of life that you feel you should have as a result of fame. Sexual love will be extremely important and intense for you, and you will need a regular partner to help reflect back to you an impression of your self in relationship. Such closer emotional experiences with lovers and children will help you to learn how to redefine your understanding of self, hopefully so that you become more inwardly settled and content. You will have to be careful to avoid domination in your relationships, either being dominated by others, or dominating them.

Natal Pluto in the 6th House

This indicates that the main compulsive tendency of Pluto will be found in the directive impulse to be of help to others, to make your life of value and purpose. This need will condition most of your actions and choices , and be a frame of reference for you when you are considering your options.

Being of use to others will provide a sense of personal satisfaction, and a meaning to your life, and essentially you will be a co-operative person. Your service to others may not always be appreciated or understood, and you will have to be careful in the ways in which you express the impulse, so that it is actually of real help and not primarily a release of your own compulsion.

Service to others can take a myriad of forms, some obvious, some more subtle, as in inner meditative work invoking spiritual energies into the world. Specialist skills and knowledge can often be applied in obvious ways, and you may feel drawn towards expressing yourself in those ways, perhaps as a teacher.

You will probably be frustrated that your efforts do not reap the sort of 'rewards or responses' that you would like to see, and that people do not usually appreciate the efforts that you make. This is inevitable, and your attitude will need adjusting to make allowances for such reactions. Looking for immediate positive response should be dropped; serving for the sake of serving and not for results should be the approach to develop: you give because it is your nature to give and because you have something of value to share. You should always review your compulsion to serve, ensuring that you are not infringing on people's individual freedom through direct interference, and that you honestly believe that what you are offering is of real value. The ways in which you try to help may require periodic adjustment, and considerable sensitivity and awareness will be needed from you when working with others.

You may find that it is more beneficial to spend time working with yourself, transforming yourself so that you can act as a channel for spiritual energies. From such a position, you would serve as a natural transmitter of the higher purpose and plan.

The sphere of health is highlighted, and you may have a talent in the healing arts; you may take further training in health matters, as a channel to serve others. It may be that problems with your health lead to changes in your basic attitudes and values, and that a transformation in your life occurs as a result of such experiences, giving your life a new direction.

It would be very meaningful for you to take employment or develop your career in a direction that you feel would be of benefit to others. This would satisfy you, giving a clear outlet for your energies, which will remain as a compulsive tendency unless you can create such a route for their healing release. Otherwise, they will stimulate an inner unease and discomfort until they are being properly used.

NATAL PLUTO IN THE 7TH HOUSE

The area of life which will require transformation, and which will have an especially deep impact upon you, is that of close and intimate relationships. The way in which you handle your relationships is the key to whether or not you will have a satisfying and emotionally complete life. If they are not carefully handled, with understanding and skill, then you are likely to experience considerable emotional pain and anguish, as your efforts repeatedly collapse into the frustrating and negative breakdown of a relationship which once offered a positive direction.

The compulsive Pluto energy will drive you towards close relations with others, and you will search for such a feeling of intensity in all your more intimate relationships. You have a need to feel that you are liked by others, and basically you will want to give a lot to others, such as making it clear that you want them to have considerable freedom in their partnership or marriage with you.

Problems can lie in an inability to live co-operatively with others, particularly as your intensity can be difficult to deal with – for you and for others. This might not even be obviously displayed, but will be sensed by others as a subtle transference of energies, which they may register as a form of manipulation or unspoken pressure on them in the relationship, struggling to reject it in some way. There are many power and energy struggles that occur in an intimate relationship that are not openly expressed between the partners, but which tend to determine its eventual success or failure.

There is an ambivalence in you towards intimacy and relationship, and much that you need to understand about yourself and others. You are simultaneously attracted to the promised intensity and a need for close partners, but also have inner fears about the power of these relations to change and redirect your life in unknown ways. Certainly, you will need to work hard on transforming aspects of yourself if a marriage or long-term partnership is to work. Any tendencies towards control over others – as a form of self-protection – should be resisted, and you may need to understand the need and discipline involved in being mutually committed to making a relationship work. It needs to work for both participants, co-operation and mutual adjustments will be required, and emotional sensitivity can be crucial. You will have to take chances with your emotions, handing your heart into the safe-keeping of another, which is probably the last thing that you really want to do, as there is a sense of unease and fear in you concerning the depths and intensity of your emotions. It would be better for you to come to an understanding of the nature of this inner intensity, and the sooner it becomes released and transformed into a conscious understanding the better you will handle this area of life.

Natal Pluto in the 8th House

This is the house of regeneration, and the transformation which Pluto seeks to bring about within you is a complex and total reorientation, concerning all levels: physical, emotional, mental and spiritual.

You are likely to use the Pluto energy in an attempt to influence the world and others to conform to your personal desires; you will use your powerful will to achieve these aims, and your persistence will erode much of the opposition that can face you.

In your relationships, you will display a tendency to manipulate others to support your purposes, and you will prefer to dominate by an insistence that others have to change in ways which are approved by you, so that they can be moulded into adjuncts of your own purpose and personality.

To further your ambitions, you will expend considerable energy in the building of a suitable platform for the expression of your underlying purpose, carefully working to a definite pattern designed to increase your influence. This can be within mainstream society, positions of authority and power, or alternatively through an exploration of the realms of the occult, which could apparently offer techniques to enhance your effectiveness.

You may become too intense and one-pointed in chasing your goals, and this could have a negative impact upon close relationships. You will have to ensure that you allow freedom for others to be themselves, just as you insist upon being yourself and following your own path; it will be more beneficial if you concentrate more on the transformation of your own self, rather than forcing others to reflect your own will.

You will be basically serious in temperament, and see life in a similar perspective, where everything is imbued with importance and meaning, but a meaning and importance which is directly related to how it affects your intentions, favourably or otherwise. You will not welcome fools or trivialities into your life, as you believe there is not the time to waste.

Sexuality is likely to be important to you, both as an energy release, and as an area in which you can exploit your power and manipulative persuasiveness. There may be compulsive elements in this aspect of your nature, and if unchecked they could lead to a damaging influence in your life unless inner changes are achieved and a reorientation is made.

Your life will be initially extremely self-centred, all absorbed into you succeeding in your chosen path, and others having to fit in accordingly. Pluto will attempt to subvert this, in order to stimulate a crisis in you, which would lead towards greater understanding and a new wholeness through releasing the driving compulsive factors. The lessons that it brings can be personally very hard, but used correctly can be extremely valuable. This subversion is likely to occur in the areas of your power and influence, marriage and sexual liaisons, the areas in which your aims are, and where you are liable to be hardest hit. Your tendency towards rigidity and self-righteousness can also be turned against you, unless you transform that pattern.

Natal Pluto in the 9th House

You will feel the need to have a strong ideological support structure guiding your life, to give it a definition, clarify your choices and offer a clear direction to follow. In many ways, your beliefs help to create your sense of personal identity, as they act as a centering energy giving a sense of solidity and permanence.

The areas which will interest you, and from which the ideological base will emerge are those of morals, ethics, politics, education, law and religion. Your social conscience and sense of responsibility will be awakened, and you may become involved with the attempt to alleviate causes of social and world problems. Certainly you will want to help in these directions, to add your contribution towards healing the ills of the world, and to oppose social hypocrisy and injustice.

Once you have adopted and established your chosen platform, you will feel a need to express it to others, and this can lead to excessive dogmatism and self-righteousness, especially in the first flush of your enthusiasm for the particular ideology. All those who possess 'the truth' or 'the right answers' suffer from this tendency to convert, convince others that theirs is the only right way. It may well be for them and an associated group, but it is most unlikely to be for everyone; not everyone accepts or believes astrology for instance.

Your intuitive abilities will lead you in a generally harmonious direction which should benefit others, and you will be ambitious to achieve success in your endeavours, possibly becoming a spokesperson for your beliefs. Much will depend upon the nature of the ideology that you adopt. Some are more inclusive than others, some can be too restrictive and limit personal freedoms; whichever you choose, it will mould your personality, so be very careful which you get involved with. At an extreme, you could become a religious fanatic, or a political revolutionary attempting to impose your perception of life upon others, expressing basically divisive attitudes into the world, as do many religious and political leaders.

The transformation which Pluto requires is for you to develop your own unique ideological approach to life, not one which relies upon following a group belief structure, and to have the strength to stand on your own feet and have the courage to follow your own path and convictions. This implies an eventual sharing with others of the individual freedom to search and discover, not merely an attempt to convert, and to encourage each to find his own unique path by releasing the need to feel secure by reflecting group beliefs uncritically and without question.

Such a new approach to the underlying tendency will act as a liberating force, potentially leading to more personal experience of the reality and validity of your essential beliefs, or to their unsuitability and failings. Pluto will act to undermine your compulsive need to adopt a structure to guide your life, by stimulating conditions that cause it to fall apart and erode your confidence in the beliefs. However, this is only because it wants to lead you towards new horizons, which are more fully expressive of your unique individuality and through which your own light can shine in freedom.

NATAL PLUTO IN THE 10TH HOUSE

The compulsive nature of the Pluto energy mediated through the 10th house focuses on the nature and expression of authority. You are likely to aspire to positions of power and authority, with the recognition that this implies. You will try to develop your natural will-power and harness it to your drive to be a success, enabling you to rise to prominence in some social or career area that you are aiming towards.

This search for authority is partially derived from a search to define your own sense of separate identity, to be known as 'someone', rather than to be an anonymous 'nobody'. You also tend to believe that those at the top are there because of right and suitability, that essentially they are superior to others, and that support of the status quo and an élitist establishment is necessary for social stability. You will be able to understand the ways of authority, and have the ability to work successfully with people in positions of power; this can aid a possible career in politics, government and local affairs involving hierarchies and bureaucracies.

If you find that you cannot personally rise to heights of social and public prestige, then you will attempt to maintain contact with those who have, so that power by association can be experienced.

Other ways to express this compulsion are either to oppose the Establishment, by having extreme revolutionary or libertarian views, or to use any influence and power that you have in order to reform existing structures of authority. The way of direct confrontation is likely to be merely a replacement of an existing system which is disliked, by a new one which is just another personal or group preference. Either is usually an imposition on the majority by a powerful minority, and historically never works as well in real life as it does in theory; and in general the new regime becomes as dictatorial as the previous one, stamping out all dissent.

Any attempt by you to initiate change will create controversy, and polarise your supporters and opponents, and you could often feel quite misunderstood. Much will depend upon how you deal with people, because that is likely to sow your seeds of future success or failure.

You will need to evaluate your personal motives and values in the light of any public fame or success, to free yourself of any glamour and illusions concerning authority and power, and from the need to tie your sense of identity in so strongly with your ambitions. Pluto, acting as a transformative and subverting energy, will use such aspects of your life to force you to discover new ways of understanding. If your personal identity is supported by being in a position of power, then be ready for Pluto to erode your influence and reputation, perhaps stripping you of it altogether. You need to have a deeper perception of the social responsibilities of authority, how to use it correctly and in a socially beneficent manner; even if the immediate sphere of influence is limited to your immediate family the same applies.

The abuse of authority is seen throughout history; the self-creation of leaders and those who follow is a common picture. To enter any 'New Age', each individual has to release his own inner light, and learn to follow his own path in co-operation with others who have achieved the same, in a unanimity of purpose and freedom – not as leaders and followers, and by the imposition of a self-serving authoritarian élite.

NATAL PLUTO IN THE 11TH HOUSE

You will find that you have a compulsive need to rely upon others, to be accepted by them as a form of validation for yourself and sense of security. Being involved with specific groups, or close associations with a large selection of friends will give a sense of definition and direction to your life. This is important to you, because it is likely that you will feel an inner impulse motivating you towards achieving specific objectives, the nature of which you do not truly grasp or understand, but which act as a magnet pulling you in their direction.

These tendencies are likely to be of a reforming nature, where your association with groups is paramount, identifying certain areas of life which you feel need to be changed for the common good, coupled with an orientation towards future life rather than an obsession with the present. You could perceive yourself as working towards securing a safer future, where the quality of life is improved for more people.

Your social ideals will be a motivating force, determining the main direction of your life, but you may need to re-evaluate certain of those group-enhanced fixed attitudes, to see if you fully agree with and support them. The problem with most ideological groups is that there is little space for, or toleration of, disagreement with the 'party line'. You will need to see how your associations with groups or friends allow you space to evolve your own thoughts and directions in the light of your own unique purpose.

Unless you are willing to conform totally to a group belief structure in order to remain in the group, you will need to develop a greater degree of self-reliance, which is much more secure and fulfilling.

As social context is important to you, you will have to ensure that your motivations are clear and realistic, and that you are not trying to take advantage of others and failing to respect their individual rights. The social idealist always desires change, change in accordance with a personal vision of an ideal world. Often this means the imposition of a personal world view upon others. This is inevitable, a part of the human process of interrelationship with the world, but one does need to understand what is occurring, and to retain a sense of humour, together with a degree of objectivity, in working towards social change.

In any intimate relationships you are liable to attempt to change a lover to suit you; but people are very resistant to change, and you could easily create extra conflict by such efforts. It is wiser to adjust to each other, whilst appreciating and enjoying the differences of the other, seeing the partnership as complementary, with change evolving naturally, rather than being forced by an insistent partner.

Pluto is likely to undermine any fixed patterns and assumed ideology that you have unthinkingly absorbed, as a result of identifying with any groups. As a result of a period of questioning this could lead you to breaking free, or having to leave, but this is inevitable if you are to discover your own light and freedom.

NATAL PLUTO IN THE 12TH HOUSE

The position of Pluto in the 12th house can be a difficult one to handle correctly; this is because areas of the personality are hidden in the unconscious mind, and yet have a potent influence creating motivations and desires which condition your life and choices.

Obviously, this applies to all Pluto placings to some extent, where the underlying impulses leading towards compulsive and repetitive action can be located in the sphere of the unconscious; but this 12th house position emphasises such influences to the point where they can almost swamp the conscious personality. The possibility of this has to be guarded against by attempts to regenerate these impulses in the unconscious, by bringing them to the surface and integrating them into the conscious mind and personality.

You will be internally preoccupied with your own mind and emotions, as though you are fascinated by the inner processes continually in motion; you can become morbidly obsessed with your own problems, and repeatedly circle around them, yet rarely facing them in an attempt to resolve and release such repetitive blockages. Traditionally, the 12th house is associated with endings and the concept of karma (the law of cause and effect, action and reaction), and you are likely to suffer from feelings of guilt and patterns of self-persecution, In some ways, you will prefer to suffer as a form of expiation for unknown sins that you feel you have committed.

Certainly, you will find it difficult to come to terms fully with yourself, and to feel an inner harmony. This is made harder by the fact that you possess a psychic sensitivity to the hidden lives of others, registering their thoughts and feelings through your links with the unconscious mind. This may manifest as confusing and conflicting thoughts, feelings and impulses arising in yourself, which may well not be yours to begin with, but someone else's being received through your sensitivity. Responding to the inner suffering of others, together with a personal sense of insecurity, can lead you to prefer more privacy and seclusion, to be free of the imposition of the social psychic atmosphere. If this process becomes understood, then a form of psychic protection could be used to minimise such intrusions, and you may find that a form of inner intuitive guidance could begin to guide your life and actions.

You may need to follow some form of path or spiritual belief which can bring some clarity into your conflicting emotional patterns; a transformation on that emotional level is essential for you, to become free of those neurotic and negative emotional guilt feelings. If that could be achieved, then your inner balance would correspondingly improve. Until such time, you will maintain a distance between yourself and others, and you may find difficulty in being able to co-operate with such a variety of personalities as you can find in the workplace. Within any intimate personal relationship, try to be as honest as possible, because in such a potentially supportive atmosphere, you may have the opportunity to allow aspects of yourself to arise from the unconscious and to deal with them through the transformatory filter of the relationship.

CHAPTER 6

Transits through the Signs and Houses

Introduction to Pluto Transits

THE TIME THAT IT TAKES FOR PLUTO to transit through all the signs of the horoscope is the longest period of any of the planets, and extends for a period of approximately 245 years, 4 months. Pluto tends to have an apparent direct motion for some seven months every year, followed by a five-month phase of retrograde motion.

Transiting Pluto aspects to natal planets, conjunction, opposition, square and trine, are likely to be made only once per planet during the individual lifetime – although, once a close aspect is made during a period of two years that aspect will be repeated some three times, or a likely five times over a three-year period. It is unlikely that transiting Pluto will conjunct all the natal planets of a person's chart.

In a normal full lifetime of 70–80 years, Pluto will only pass through between three and six of the signs, and the amount will be determined by the natal sign at birth; if it is between Leo and Aquarius, then five or six signs will be transited during the life, and if between Aquarius and Cancer perhaps only three or four.

The time that Pluto takes to pass through the signs is as follows: Aries and Gemini, 30 years; Taurus, 31 years; Cancer and Pisces 25 years; Leo and Aquarius, 19 years; Virgo and Libra, 14 years; Scorpio, 12 years; Sagittarius and Capricorn, 13 years.

It is interesting to consider those signs in which Pluto remains the longest, and those where the stay is shorter. Aries, Taurus,

Gemini and Cancer span a period of 116 years, and tend to indicate a grounding of the new Pluto impulse for that cycle. Aries releasing the seed of a new impulse into society, Taurus beginning to earth it into a solid foundation, Gemini seeing it anchored within responsive minds, and the early evidence of its implications being disseminated via social communication, and Cancer absorbing it into an emotional desire for it to happen socially, and a clash centred around the needs for security.

The shorter span signs of Leo to Capricorn, covering some 85 years, see the root being established within society, making its impact, creating adherents of support and reactionary enemies of opposition as the evolutionary progression strives to move onwards. By the time it reaches Aquarius, a group embodiment of the impulse has been created, ensuring its perpetuation into the next cycle, and acknowledgement and acceptance of the purposeful thrust of the impulse is clear, even if still only to a receptive minority.

In Pisces, the ending of the cycle occurs, with further stages of dissolution of the old order and its replacement by the new creating social conflicts, ready for the next cycle to be energised.

The gestation period can easily take a century before the new way can be clearly seen and identified, following the period of below-ground activity. Achieving success with the impulse may well take several cycles to pass, each making some definite progress in modifying society sufficiently to enable it to absorb fully the extensive vision of which Pluto is the overseer.

Most of us will have been born after the Pluto–Cancer transit at the eve of the First World War, and so our lives will be overshadowed by the phase of social conflict and the dissemination throughout society of the potential of new ways of living and thinking, attempts to overthrow the old order by the new. For those responding to the new progressive energies, social commitment and responsibility is made to the new gods and vision, and the unfoldment of this is indicated in the section of Pluto transiting through the signs. This is our collective participation and sacrifice to the rising Phoenix.

The social impact of Pluto moving through the signs is dramatic, stimulating the fall of outmoded social structures and their replacement by new ones. Its immediate impact is dualistic – negative and positive, yet its effects are always permanent in nature. Once it begins to erode the cohesiveness of its chosen target, then its ending is inevitable, despite attempts to restore its former glories: Pluto is not sentimental!

For the individual, Pluto often has disturbing effects, shaking the status quo and not allowing the illusion of real security to be believed in. Because its transits through the signs and houses go on for so long, its influence may not always be openly apparent; but it seems that in many ways it underpins all transits made by the other transpersonal planets. It sets a tone which is constantly present, into which all the incidental social developments concomitant with the transits of the other planets are eventually absorbed, supporting players to the hidden Pluto purpose.

As Pluto transits through a third to a half of the houses, those that it enters are especially highlighted and important to the development of that individual, being intensely vitalised and energised. The houses indicate that Pluto seeks to bring about a radical change in that sphere of the individual life, a new way of experiencing or perceiving that field of human existence, where attitudes can be transformed, or new creative qualities unfolded, or where change needs to dissolve an impending stagnation of the spirit. It is a forcing process, where there is a disidentification, chosen or enforced, with previous fixed personal or social allegiances; a dethroning of the old kings, and a breaking down of the pressure and power of the collective values, beliefs and attitudes. For those who consciously respond to the Pluto energy, and for those who attempt to oppose it, Pluto is a very demanding god, striking a hard bargain for his gifts, and never accepting no for an answer.

Life is an ongoing process, and transits are an integral influence upon that inner clock ticking away, like an inner time-keeper. We only have a choice in the way in which we respond to change occurring; we cannot oppose change itself. It is much more beneficial to choose to respond positively to Pluto transits, to accept the fact that change is necessary in some sphere that Pluto is entering or is present within. A conscious decision to work with the energy will make it easier to transform, rather than having to endure the pressure of external events forcing the process. To be an unconscious victim of life processes is not recommended; a willing co-participant is much more rewarding and healthy.

These house transits are quite broad and embracing, and always reflect deep-seated difficulties in achieving the transformational breakthrough that appears to be required. They can be very painful and prolonged, almost as if all aspects of the self are being

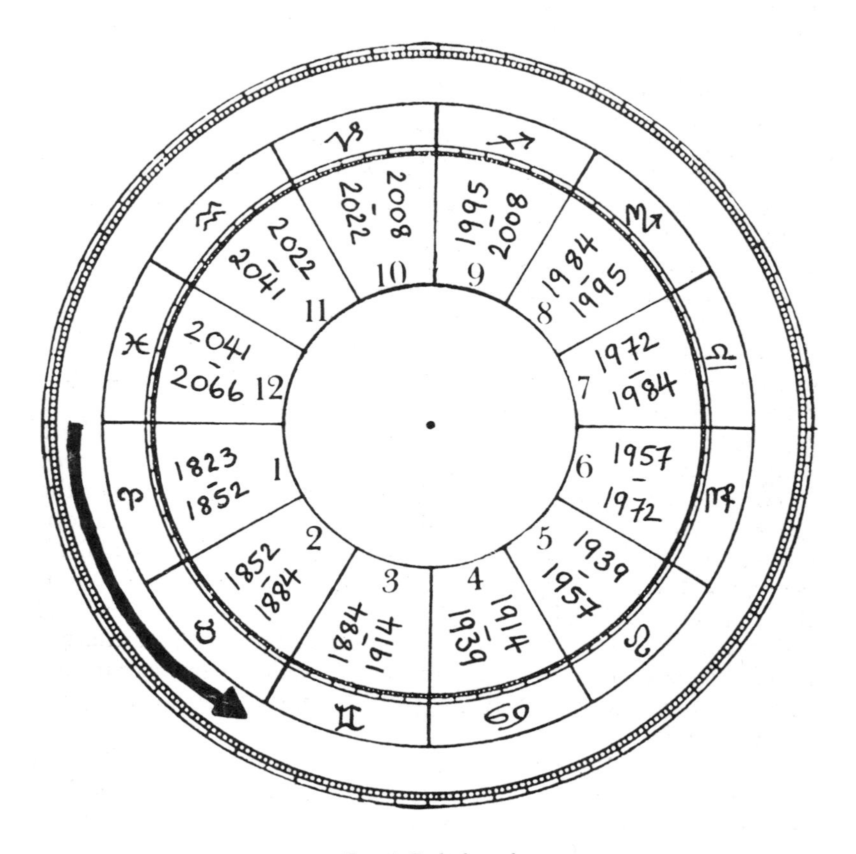

Transit Cycle through
Signs and Houses

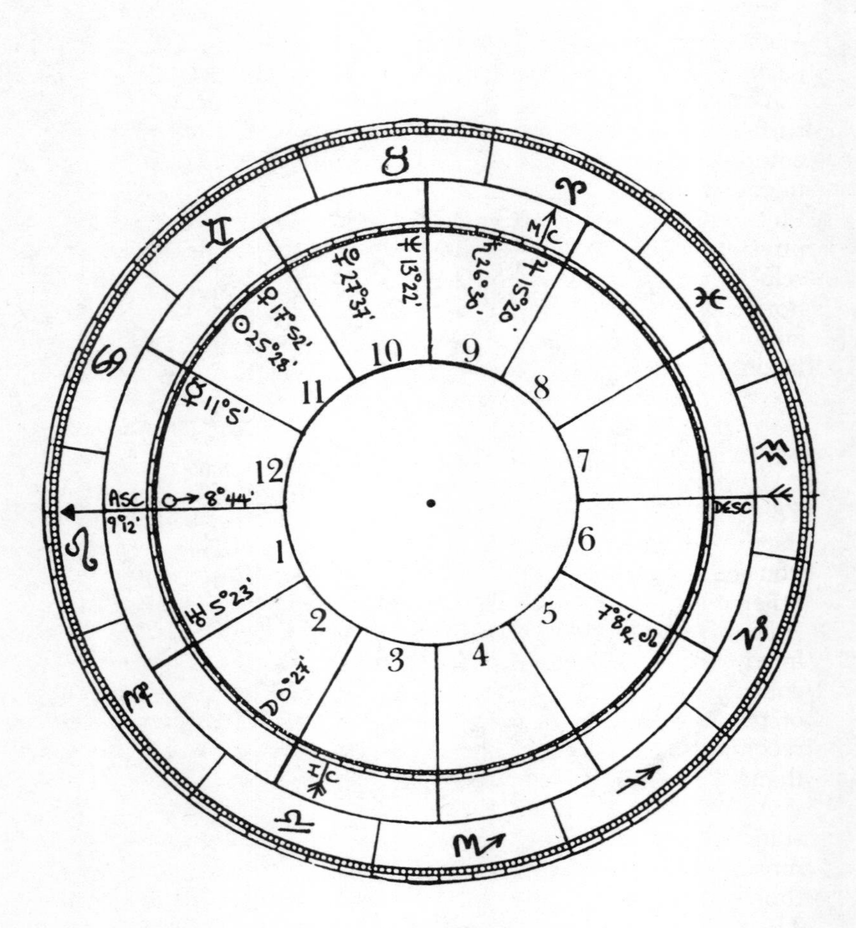

Alice A. Bailey
Founder of Lucis Trust/
Arcane School
Pluto Trine Moon
Square Uranus
Natal Pluto 10th House

tested and reassembled. The particular house gives the surface sphere of life to be changed, but in fact the changes demanded cut across all aspects of the life.

These changes could easily be a development in building your own unique perspective and understanding of life, to become more whole in yourself, able to emerge from the cocoon of the collective society of received attitudes, values and beliefs. This is very difficult, and often traumatic in nature. Usually, the sensation is of aloneness and isolation, irrespective of any support from others which you are fortunate enough to have. It is that you realise that your inner change is deeply personal to yourself, and that no one can really support you as you pass through this metamorphosis. It is a stage of the regenerative rising of the Phoenix, a refining experience and a coming to terms with the contradictory composite self. For instance, a 1st house Pluto transit will involve a dissolving of the current sense of personal identity and a hoped for reassembly into greater wholeness. This can involve the eliminative purging of all those psychological wastes that have accumulated over time, in order to re-establish a healthy inner balance; a state of constipation is not exclusively a physical phenomenon.

The natal position of Pluto indicates what can be considered to be a lifetime challenge for the individual, a crucial area of life that needs regeneration in some way, and which becomes a yardstick for an evaluation of 'growth and success'. As the transits proceed through their particular spheres which also require a lesser transformation, they also act as a channel towards the resolution of the natal challenge too. Progress and growth in the transit spheres leads to a corresponding movement to achieve the natal regeneration. This intimate link should be noted and considered, so that from within any inner turmoil, a direction of resolution for the future takes shape.

At the time of the Pluto transits, whether it is moving into a new house or sign, or making a close aspect with a natal planet, there is a distinct release of vibrant energy from the unconscious. This is stimulatory and often has the effect of awakening dormant memories which may have been forgotten or repressed, or inhibited behavioural or personality patterns. What seems to arise into the mind are aspects of the self or experiences that may hold some meaningful insight into the individual nature or future life. It seems to be intended that in some way they are to be consciously worked with, as an integrative process through which a confrontation with repressed experiences can become an act of self-healing.

There will always be an emotional dimension to the area that Pluto is stimulating, and it is this that will be the source of most of the pain and discomfort that can ensue when inner conflict is occurring. Forms of emotional agitation, instability and inner tension are to be expected as Pluto brings a phase to a close and prepares to open a new cycle. It seems to be quite common that people experience greater awareness of personal mortality at these times, sometimes through the death of someone they know, sometimes just by the inner Plutonic process triggering the mind to feel the shadow of death's inevitability. This awareness alone can lead to great changes in some lives, as people question the way that they are living their lives and their personal fulfilment in life. Often they discover that they would rather be using their limited time in other ways, and can begin to transform their lives accordingly.

For some, Pluto transits will reinvigorate their emotions. Often, under the pressures of life, people tend to inhibit their emotional responses, especially men, and live without acknowledging the values of that aspect of themselves. Pluto can cause uncontrollable passions to arise, a bursting of the inhibiting dam walls, and this can obviously create problems in relatively stable lives; perhaps as middle-aged men or women embark on dangerous affairs, or feel that in some way they have to 'prove themselves' in some context or reassert individual identity or attractiveness. The sense of personal identity can often be affected by the abrasive Pluto energy, where those social masks begin to crack and fall away, along with a multitude of pretences and illusions about themselves, others and the way life is often lived. Once that fundamental disillusionment occurs, the difficulty lies in deciding what to do next, because the old way of living has been destroyed, and the falsity of it cannot be rebuilt.

Pluto through the Signs

PLUTO IN ARIES (1823-1852)

This is the initial impulse of the new cycle of Pluto transiting through the signs. It is a time of new beginnings, a time of the sowing of new seeds to initiate the conditioning patterns which will work their way through into manifestation in the world during the following 250 years.

Pluto is sometimes considered to be a joint ruler of Aries with Mars, and the transformatory effects of Pluto in this sign will be expressed via the Arian qualities of fiery energy and enthusiasm released in an aggressive and direct manner. The key to the Aries energy is the need to assert the personal self through action, to act as an initiator of new projects and directions to take in life. Self is experienced and confronted by personally created challenges, in order to realise the individual state of 'I Am'.

This often leads towards action and movement purely as a release from inner tension created by the Arian energy, often taken without due thought and consideration for the eventual results of such activity. Impatience and impulsiveness are likely to lead towards future problems and uncompleted activities.

This phase ushered in a period of world exploration and individual pioneering, as the Victorian empire began to expand across the world, and the Europeans began to colonise and explore the continent of North America. The new cycle of seeding for the future had begun. The influence of the English culture, language and way of life was physically grafted onto foreign cultures by the export of imperialism backed by force of arms. Explorers like David Livingstone in Africa were a symbol of Arian activity in penetrating new areas of potential opportunity. Any far corner of the world was fair game for the expansionary impulse.

North American wilderness areas were a target for the intrepid explorers, who were trying to forge a new nation and a new life for themselves. Attracted by the promise of a way of living based on freedom and individual choice, an increasing number of Europeans crossed the Atlantic in their search for new opportunities and adventure. In Europe, new revolutionary movements arose, as in France and Italy in 1848, aiming to overthrow the regimes in power and existing monarchies. Such movements were fired by the need to assert individual freedoms and confront the older established orders, to bring the people to power and to destroy the ruling élites. These forms of activity were an expression of the transforming effect of Pluto when mediated through the tendencies of Aries. The new seeding was designed to trigger a new era of self-discovery for the individual, and to lead towards greater knowledge and conscious integration of the many countries and races in the world. Obviously, this process is still occurring, but this phase was the new impulse for the present Pluto cycle, which lasts almost until 2070, and the subsequent sign transits of Pluto develop this initial course.

PLUTO IN TAURUS (1852–84)

The underlying impulse of this phase was the need to establish a sense of rootedness, of societal stability based upon firm foundations and a distinct way of behaviour derived from the 'social class' of the individual as evidenced in Victorian England.

The prime area of expression was the emphasis upon material productivity, material acquisitions and a better quality of life. This was developed from the deeper integration into society of the impact of the 'new technology' arising from the European Industrial Revolution, and the greater use of machines as creators of enhanced productivity. It was a period of great economic expansion in Europe, and led to the building of a world-wide export and import market and international trade. These early steps towards a world economic system, where nations grew to become more interdependent both as suppliers and consumers of goods and raw materials, led towards new international friendships and alliances and also increased friction between economic rivals who were competing in the same marketplaces.

The generational response to the mediating Taurus energy was aimed at conquering the earth and matter. The urge was to discover and to use in a practical way those essential energies locked away as secrets within matter. The need was for practical efficiency, and answers to the mysteries of life that were especially tangible and concrete. This led to the theory of evolution as proposed by Darwin, which seemed to provide an answer to the question of man's origins, as well as to the development of a scientific materialism and view of life which saw the universe as a machine and not as living organism. These attitudes are still very prevalent in mainstream thinking today.

The key to this combination of energies, of Pluto and Taurus, is the theme of personal possession, where security is primarily looked for in material possessions, which give physical comfort and a pleasurable satisfaction in ownership. This enhanced the need for consumer productivity and gave an impetus towards the later technological revolution of the twentieth century. The trend in society was to give priority to the material tools of productivity, and to ideas that could be practically applied. The flow of societal energy was directed externally towards the achieving of the new material goals; there was little time or energy left for an inner analysis of what the society was beginning to identify with – the emerging god of materialism.

This tendency is exemplified by the evaluation and interpretation of human life and social meaning in terms of economic theory and the raising of the concept of 'state' into greater dominance. In 1869 Karl Marx published his *Das Kapital*, the influence of which is still very powerful today with the eventual development of Communism and socialism. By 1871, the most dynamic political force in Europe was nationalism, stimulated and reflected by the successful efforts of Bismarck in uniting the German states.

It is of interest to note two examples of the subversive effect of Pluto. Darwin's evolutionary theory undermined the hold of the Church on society's thinking, challenging the fundamentalist and literalist biblical attitudes of the time. From that time on, the Church would lose its stranglehold on minds to be replaced by a new priesthood of scientific materialism. Parallel to the fading of the Church's influence, the Western mental culture was impregnated by the seeds of Eastern metaphysical philosophies. Madame Blavatsky and her Theosophical Society were prime movers in this process, which was seeking to introduce a new vision of God and man's role in the world and universe which would be more apt for the changing time and the future than that of the existing Church. The influence of these seeds is yet to be fully realised and seen in the world.

PLUTO IN GEMINI (1884–1914)

During this period, the dawn of the modern world of international communication and travel was built upon new progress in the realms of science and technology, which was entering a phase of rapid expansion in knowledge and practical applications. Especially important were the investigations into the uses of electrical power and technology, by people like Edison, Bell and Tesla. This would lay the foundations for the future reliance of our contemporary technological state on electrical energy, operating through our mass communications and computer systems, and in all aspects of modern life.

Gemini is associated with mind, intellect and communication, and apart from the increasing reliance upon an electrical technology, there was also the development of new forms of physical transport which would become extremely important in the building of our modern international societies. These were the mechanical creations of the automobile and the early aeroplanes (with first flights by 1903), both of which would play roles in the First World War. These began to offer a new freedom of mobility for people, and offered the potential to expand man's physical and mental horizons.

Gemini's orientation towards mind encouraged intellectual curiosity and a thirst for knowledge. A phase of nonconformism and artistic freedom began to occur amongst those searching for new horizons, as Gemini prefers to maintain its unique individuality. These are the early signs of a movement seeking to break away from the materialistic preoccupations and social structures of the previous Taurus transit towards more mobile individual freedom.

The development and increasing use of telephones, automobiles and air travel began to create a shrinking world, despite the strongly nationalistic attitudes still prominent in all countries. This was a phase where the analytical mind grew more important, where there was a striving for everything to be identified and classified, and where speech and the written word were often seen as the essential vehicles of communication. The process of analysis begun by Gemini is still paramount today, leading in an ever more complex world towards more confusion derived from its basic divisive attitudes. What is needed is a process of synthesis, the creation of intelligible whole systems to enable a holistic understanding to occur. Analysis is only half of the story; synthesis is required for completeness.

The role of Pluto here is to trigger a new system of world communications, to unify an awareness of one world, and potentially to break down all separative barriers between people, locally, nationally and internationally. The introduction of cars and planes demonstrates the always ambiguous effects of Pluto. Socially creative and positive, leading to an increase in personal freedoms, yet also leading towards the creation of other social dangers and problems. Excessive car fumes, landscapes redesigned for car travelling; the development of planes into nuclear missiles, and computer communications leading towards Star Wars. There is also the emigration of people to new countries which offer a better life, creating racial and immigration difficulties as the races physically mix and merge in multiracial countries.

Pluto seems to point towards an envisaged future, guiding individuals and groups in forming the essential building blocks of the new society, yet hiding the knowledge of the problems that will be self-created by the decisions of humanity, and the difficult challenges in national and international unification that are required to achieve the golden vision. It forces mankind in certain directions, often appearing to be inevitable, often painful, forcing change.

The Gemini phase ended at the eve of the First World War, a real and negative initial response to the seeding of the mental vision of one world.

PLUTO IN CANCER (1914–1939)

During this Cancer phase, the reactions to the stresses and tensions of the slow movement towards the embodiment of the Pluto vision for the total cycle began to erupt in the European industrial nations.

Cancer is a sign associated with domesticity, emotional feelings and sentiment, and is intimately connected with a sense of security, which it seeks to find in its immediate environment or possession of land. This impulse began to stimulate those more self-centred separatist attitudes, creating a strong nationalistic movement in each nation across the world, where the unique qualities and characteristics of each nation were highlighted and emphasised. Underlying the nationalistic attitudes was an unhealthy degree of emotional fanaticism looking for an excuse to burst through into public action. National boundaries and sense of identity became more important for the well-being of the people, and the concepts of 'motherland and fatherland' came into greater prominence.

The environment began to be changed due to new agricultural techniques, chemicals were used on the land to stimulate growth, and water-damming was applied to create hydroelectric power. Improved transport meant that agricultural produce could be moved more easily across the country to distant markets. Farming began to change from small-scale production to a system of large-scale, nationally orientated concerns with capital to buy extra land and new technology for greater productivity.

Undermining any sense of security was economic instability and international struggle. In America there was the Wall Street Crash; in Germany, escalating inflation had by 1923 created the platform for National Socialism to emerge, and in Britain and America the Great Depression of 1929 led to thousands being out of work and in poverty. In Russia, the fall of the Tsar's regime and the Revolution of 1917 would be of world importance.

It is during the time period of this transit that Pluto was 'discovered', and the movement through Cancer appears to have stimulated several important movements in twentieth-century history. In 1919, the League of Nations was formed as a precursor to the later United Nations, the aim of which is to encourage world nations to work together in peace for the good of all men; and in the same year there was the establishment of the Fascist and Nazi parties in Italy and Germany. In 1923, *Mein Kampf* was published, coinciding with rampant inflation in Germany and the growth of Hitler's influence and that of the Nazis. In Italy, Mussolini was dictator by 1925. In Russia, Stalin had gained power by 1929. All of these charismatic, ruthless leaders seem to have been capable of 'feeding off' the Pluto energy, using it with great efficiency to build social and political power, yet also being inwardly warped by its negative use, which eventually led to their downfall.

The subversive Pluto energy is especially potent in this Cancer phase. Despite the Cancerian need for security, the Pluto influence leads to entirely the opposite. There was little peace or stability in the world from 1914 to 1945, and it appears as if Pluto was trying to speed the changes along, and bring in several elements that are destined to be major players in the remainder of the cycle. In response to those social and economic pressures, and the increasing fears in individuals and society of impending collapse, new approaches to government began to appear in the main Western nations. In America, the 'New Deal' concept emerged, in Europe, Fascism, and in Russia, Communism. As a result of the First World War, the more traditional foundations of family and national lifestyles began to undergo considerable change, especially as many families had lost men in the war. This led to the change in role of women in society, an expansion of their traditional functions and status.

An extremely hard lesson was faced by the world in 1945. If the nations insisted upon the maintenance and emphasis on partisan politics, isolationalism and nationalistic and racist attitudes which lacked a spirit of unity, then the security that people looked for would never occur. Instead there would be friction between nations, and potentially devastating wars reflecting the deep disharmony between people. The challenge was to change society and the people so that a way forward to real security could be found. The end of the Cancer phase saw the emergence of a group in Germany who embodied an old way of thinking in the world – Hitler and the National Socialist Party – who by invoking nationalistic dreams and attitudes, a destiny of a thousand-year Reich, and the concept of the pure Aryan superman, plunged the world into its second world war in twenty-five years. The clash of the old and the new energies, old and new gods, Cancer and Pluto.

PLUTO IN LEO (1939–57)

This phase is of extreme importance in the unfolding of the Pluto cycle, being pivotal in the scientific release of atomic energy and the international effects of that knowledge, creating a world challenge that is still to be faced and correctly understood.

Initially, this transit opened with the world entering again into a new world war, stimulated by over-exaggerated national pride and expansionist tendencies, looking for ways to flex economic and military muscles in an aggressive manner. Leo is a sign of leadership and kingship, and this period saw the exploitation of power through political dictatorships in Europe, such as those of Hitler and Mussolini, who came into the public eye during the Cancer transit, but by now had attained the peak of their power.

The more negative aspects of dictator power are displayed, such as extreme political ruthlessness in ensuring their social control, and in totalitarian tendencies and suppression of dissent. The combination of the Leo and Pluto energies led to problems in the right handling of personal/national power. This enhanced national selfishness stirred the passions of ancient group assertiveness and violence, and amplified the nationalistic attitudes of élitist superiority.

Pluto is exalted in the sign of Leo, a Fire sign, and the new atomic energy was discovered and used to speed the end of the Second World War. This gave mankind the ability to destroy the race and the planet, if it so chooses. The more negative face of the Pluto vision is thus demonstrated as potential planetary destruction; the underlying positive vision is planetary unity and the creative human-centred uses of scientific knowledge. The issue is personal and national use of power, whether to be used for the good of all, or for selfish purposes and self-aggrandisement.

As a result of the war, the colonial empires of the Western nations began to break down, and new independent states emerged. The creation of Israel in 1948 led to Middle Eastern tensions and Arab–Israeli conflicts; and a new form of nationalism grew, committed to throwing off the yoke of colonial oppression and reclaiming national identity: witness the case of India, which became free of British control in 1947.

The post-war years saw the creation or renewal of several idealistic organisations. The failed League of Nations was reborn under the broader concept of the United Nations in 1945, and the European Economic Community was established between 1955 and 1957, joining nations together for mutual benefit. In Britain, socialist ideals were established by policies involving a Welfare State, a National Health Service and a new education system based more on ability than on class divisions. A new People's Republic emerged in China in 1949, based upon Communist principles, and at the end of the transit, the exploration of space was inaugurated with the launching of Sputnik in 1957.

The struggle for world domination, to be 'king of the jungle' became polarised between two great states (supported by their allies). This was the continuing struggle between two differing political systems and ideologies, of capitalism as embodied in America, and of Communism in the Soviet Union. These two great economic and military powers confront each other across the world, using surrogate nations as their fields of conflict. It appears that if these two states could become reconciled, and reduce the chances of a planetary nuclear war, then the unifying vision of Pluto would come much closer to manifestation. This seems to be the route indicated.

PLUTO IN VIRGO (1957–72)

This phase saw the world recovering from the ravages of war, and focused upon material reconstruction and progress. Virgo is an Earth sign, and this will be mainly associated with matter and concerns of a practical nature. Pluto's influence is apparent in the changes which began to occur in the spheres of personal health, employment and industry, all things which have a pronounced conditioning effect on the quality of the material lifestyles of people.

This was the beginning of the computer age, which now affects most aspects of life. Business, industry and the military were early users of this new technology. Meanwhile, increasing automation in factories and offices began to de-skill and wipe out jobs, replacing people with machines.

Medical care and knowledge, plus multi-national pharmaceutical companies, helped to raise the quality of life for many in the West; although by the 1980s, certain attitudes and techniques of the medical profession were being questioned as to their real efficacy. The dangers of chemical pollution and side-effects began to lead to a renewal of interest in older health approaches, and natural foods and alternative therapies began to proliferate.

At this time, there was a growing awareness of the trend of materialistic science to lead humanity towards dangers: nuclear and environmental hazards, and social dehumanisation. The generation born during the Leo transit, with its emphasis upon individualism, triggered off the 'cult of the young' with the birth and world-wide influence of rock'n'roll, the Beatles and the Hippy movement during the sixties.

The influence of the 'new music' allied to new fashions, new lifestyle attitudes, and a questioning rejection of traditional social conduct and beliefs has led to many changes in society, and greater freedom for individual expression. The release of consciousness-changing psychedelic drugs has been a major influence on many millions of people born after the end of the war. These drugs provided different ways of self-experience and perception of life and the universe to those who experimented with them. The Hippies' response to the Pluto energy was to proclaim 'Make love not war', a profound life-affirming and transformatory attitude, quite in harmony with the planetary vision yet falling foul of a naive expression and a cynical society that even now cannot accept the real sense of that alternative. On a world scale the Hippies briefly flowered as a simple expression of one way of living the Pluto vision, but 'died' due to world resistance, and their own inability to transform themselves without the aid of eventually negative drugs.

Simultaneous with the inner exploration of space through drugs, man succeeded in breaking free of the planetary confines by exploring outer space and the moon landings. This also provided the world with the image of planet Earth, as photographed by the astronauts, suspended as a globe in space. This is an extremely important image, displaying one Earth, and is the pictorial symbol of the Pluto vision, the transpersonal understanding.

Effective forms of birth control were developed, leading to choice in creating families and the sudden arising of a new sexual freedom and morality. The nuclear family concept began to break down under the new pressures in society; sexual and moral pressures, an increased work mobility, and a desire for individual life choice all helped to increase opportunities and personal freedoms from the restrictions of the established social attitudes. Most aspects of life were suitable for challenging, and personal rejections of a machine-like lifestyle became more common as a search for a better, more unique quality of life increased.

The Virgo tendencies towards a narrowness of outlook, and an analytical approach which sought knowledge in order to bring matter under the control of mind, was subverted by the Pluto influence. This was attempting to demonstrate that mind is a good servant but a dangerous master, unless it is balanced by an awareness of a global purpose and regard for the value and quality of human life.

PLUTO IN LIBRA (1972–84)

The image of Libra is the scales of balance, which are rarely in equilibrium or harmony, but are usually out of balance in disharmony. In those individual lives with a strong Libran influence, as well as in the lives of nations, the Libran energy appears to be difficult to handle positively and in a consistent manner.

This phase, saw the beginning of a movement in politics and society against certain of the more libertarian personal freedoms that has been shaking societies in previous years. A backlash effect began to occur against trade union power, sexual freedom and the 'permissive society', individual lifestyle choice, spiritual movements and sects, creative education, etc. There was a hankering after a return to a 'golden past', when life was socially predictable and people basically followed the socially acceptable patterns of life, and 'morals ruled' under the controlling hand of a political élite of those who felt sure that they knew what was right for everyone. Essentially, it was a reaction towards the recent speed of change in the world, which was and still is, intensifying.

What Pluto is attempting to indicate through Libra is the urgent need for greater co-operation and sense of world responsibility and interdependence. Human relationships on a personal and world stage are the key to the future; if they are self-centred and separatist, then pain and suffering become eventually inevitable, or if a form of group consciousness of fellow members of one human race can become more dominant, then a more positive and peaceful future would be assured. Again, Pluto emphasises the nature of the choice facing mankind. A global vision needs to be seeded, and seen as the real alternative and path to take.

Certainly, by the 1980s, we have global problems where the use of new technology and energy sources creates environmental pollution, is negatively affecting traditional employment patterns and trade, and creating areas where hunger, violence and societies bent on virtual self-destruction are common. In this negative sense, the world is more one world than it ever has been before. What has to be realised and properly learnt before it is too late, is that division will only lead to disaster and suffering, and that the only hope lies in unity; this is just a pragmatic realisation and an expression of common sense.

In Libra, the past and future ways begin to confront each other again, and the polarity between the 'good old times' attitudes and those which are future-orientated grows more stark. In this period, Fundamentalism began to grow in strength in the Middle East and in America, with the new Islamic Republics in the Middle East and born-again Christians in America, echoed by the return to Victorian values in Thatcher's Britain. It is a re-evaluation of the past, clashing with the needs of the future world, and is an underlying theme to this phase. In the USSR, Communism began to undergo change, as the older established political leaders began to fade away. Similarly, China at this time embarked on a new approach incorporating aspects of Western capitalism grafted onto a Communist system, which could potentially offer a new meeting-place for the two opposing ideologies to meet and join together.

This period was a time of world economic uncertainty, when the impact of new technology began to be felt on employment levels, and across the Western world many millions became unemployed and alienated from the consumer society by financial hardship. It is a transition period, the dying of old industries and old ways of production, and the new forms of replacement are still being born or have to become socially acceptable first. A questioning of social values increases, especially certain scientific trends which have negative effects on the well-being of life and people, and a search by many for those which enhance the positive qualities of life, a search for the right direction to take.

PLUTO IN SCORPIO (1984–95)

During this transit, the Pluto energies are being transmitted to the world through the sign with which they have most affinity, Scorpio. This means that the energies will be at their least diluted, and will almost certainly pose difficult challenges for humanity to face. The resulting success or failure will largely determine the shape of the remainder of the Pluto cycle through to Pisces.

It is likely that the speed of world change will accelerate even more, and that nations will respond with confusion and outdated thinking to the inevitable changes being stimulated in a multiplicity of ways by Pluto. World tension will increase and armed conflict will often prove irresistible, especially in Third World countries and the Middle East, which are already unstable areas. In view of this, it is essential that the superpowers avoid becoming embroiled in more direct conflict in surrogate countries.

Scorpio and Pluto are transformative energies, and the themes of rebirth, regeneration and renewal allied to a period of endings and new creation are the dominant keynotes. The world is faced with global problems, which are not really being resolved yet, as the 'world leaders' and politicians still express old attitudes conditioned by dangerous separatist thinking. This has to change as the Piscean Age fades away, and mankind moves towards its self-judgement day, reaping the consequences of its choices. Whilst it may appear negative, it is likely that the greatest dangers will face humanity in this phase, and the only recourse is for planetary unity to occur and a radical shift in the world state of mind. Dangers particularly involve nuclear war, famine, plague and environmental pollution. One danger facing the world is the increase in sexually transmitted diseases, especiallly AIDS, which is a prime example of Pluto/Scorpio working through the sex-drive, and apparently undermining several of the individual freedoms already brought through since Pluto in Virgo. These include the development of homosexual rights and the acceptance of homosexuals by society, and that of sexual permissiveness; both of these are now being questioned due to the spread of AIDS. A return to older attitudes is not the way forward, but a new and deeper understanding of the sexual impulse and energy needs to emerge.

Essentially, the world has to take positive steps towards embodying the concept of the planetary village, the commonality and value of the human life irrespective of race, colour or creed, uniting in tolerance, understanding and brotherhood. It is likely that a new evolutionary and revolutionary impulse will be released during this period, expressed with a universal perspective, and backed by occult forces. Certainly there will be an increase in concern for the planet, and the collective influence of environmentalists will increase in value. Ideally, what should come through is a new form of politics to lead into the Aquarian age, one which builds a bridge resolving the present problems and creates a platform for social transformation and global awareness. The new politics will be human-centred, where the good of the individual is also good for the world; it would be very radical, yet would possess the key to guarantee a future if it can be transmitted through into manifestation, whereas the existing social and political models are unable to change and break the patterns of conflict and confrontation inherent in them.

Pluto in Scorpio confronts man with the reality of the world that he has made; the dark side of man is sufficient to destroy the world, and this energy will definitely stimulate the shadow-self, but ideally in order to redeem itself and become reborn into greater light. The old order breaks down, and like the Phoenix, the new is reborn from the ashes of the old.

PLUTO IN SAGITTARIUS (1995–2008)

The positive effects of this transit are dependent upon the progress made by humanity during the Scorpio crisis and turning point. The energies of Sagittarius emphasise the fields of religion, law, education and travel, philosophical idealism and a need for considerable personal liberty and freedom.

Such tendencies will have a natural influence upon the spheres of religion and politics. In the world of religion, the existing religious beliefs will be questioned more, as a new religious impulse begins to enter society, which is more inclusive, understanding and modern. A new formulation of the religious impulse is necessary for a new world, one which reflects the essential spiritual values and sense of direction for humanity, yet which does not alienate people through the maintenance of archaic and socially dangerous beliefs. The new religion is intended to be founded upon personal experience of the spiritual realities, rather than upon blind faith and surrender to the dictates of a spiritual priesthood.

In the contemporary world, many aspects of the existing world religions are unsuitable, and most of them are in the final phase of their natural life-span; a synthesis of their common and essential roots is the initial step forward, leading potentially towards one world religion. This will include modern scientific belief and knowledge in a new understanding of the need of humanity for spiritual meaning in life, because both approach the mystery of life from two different but complementary perspectives, and a common ground can be established by a unification of the two mental attitudes.

The Sagittarian search for liberty and freedom could stimulate change in any country which is restricting personal freedoms, and new ideologies devoted to appeal to people will arise, guided by leaders who are responding to that impulse. This is likely to lead towards inner conflict in repressive regimes.

By the end of this phase, it is expected that the new social threads of politics, religion and science will be more intertwined in a new globally responsible pattern, and that the thrust of the world direction will be moving towards the Aquarian vision. If progress is not made, then the foundations of the world society will be shaking under the reaction to the pressure for change; and what may arise is a negative distortion of the positive approach, with authoritarian religion supporting increasingly totalitarian regimes, and creating a diminution of individual freedoms and the likelihood of international conflict.

PLUTO IN CAPRICORN (2008–2022)

Capricorn is an Earth sign, and during this phase, there will be a conflict between those entrenched social, political and economic structures and those which are trying to emerge as suitable replacements capable of mediating the new ideas and directions of the transpersonal vision.

The necessity for new political structures should be obvious in most nations by this time, the main questions being the clarification of the direction to move towards, and the nature of the new structures to achieve the new aims. The need for global responsibility and national interdependence will be dominant, and each nation will need to develop a planetary attitude, whilst ensuring that its own unique racial identity is valued and integrated in a global tapestry of unified vision.

Crystallised structures in politics and business will be liable to be eroded by Pluto's action, and old ways of thinking will be clearly perceived as inadequate to solve social problems. The seed of the new visionary ideal will permeate the world mind of humanity, and the will to earth this approach becomes inexorable, even at the cost of additional social strain and global tension, as existing patterns of life are questioned. More people consciously support the new ideals, and act as a transmitting agency into the world.

During the last Pluto/Capricorn transit, new concepts of government were released, the main one in the 'new world of America', with the famous Declaration of Independence in 1776 and the basic concepts of Western democracy and the rights and freedoms of man being established.

It would be an appropriate time for a more effective form of world government to be born. The current United Nations is a basic model, but will always be inadequate until the nations are willing to co-operate positively on a global platform of the greatest good for humanity. Whilst they mainly act in power blocs against other opposing groupings, disunity is to be expected; however, when the need for world unity becomes paramount, then the initial stage of working co-operatively together becomes inevitable for mutual benefit and the situation will change.

As Capricorn is a sign associated with authority and leadership, some countries may initially react by trying to impose strong authoritarian regimes on their people. Pluto will undermine any such attempts, and based on the development of the previous Sagittarian transit and its essential urge towards greater freedoms, there will be groupings of people in all nations dedicated to subverting such governmental tendencies. This may lead to international tension, but it is expected that by this time the USSR will have elements of democracy and capitalism integrated into its own unique Communist structure, thus creating a regenerated political system which can more easily enter into dialogue and co-operation with the West. This will remove the major threat to world peace, and it can be hoped that by working together to secure peace, the superpowers will be able to act as supports in a changing world, as living symbols of how opposites can mutually exist in harmony.

PLUTO IN AQUARIUS (2022–2041)

The image of Aquarius is the Water-bearer, the container and releaser of the potent life energy present in the water. As is well known, we stand at the threshold of the new Age of Aquarius, so it is reasonable to assume that this transit of Pluto through Aquarius will be very influential. It is likely to sound the death knell of the old civilisation, and to see the formative seeds of the new cycle displaying early shoots above the ground and putting down roots for the new world, Also at this time there will be seeds sown which will not emerge from the ground until much later in the cycle. Such later seeds could be foreseen as a future vision by those in society who can register the inner pattern unfolding as life on earth.

Aquarius is a sign associated with individuality, universal brotherhood and group consciousness, and is an Air sign stimulating mind and the intellect. Scientific developments are likely to be made during this phase, which are directly linked to the needs of the future cycle, and to the furtherance of world humanitarianism.

The previous Pluto/Aquarius transit saw the development of a free democratic state in America, the Constitution and Bill of Rights, and the French Revolution, with its ideal embodied in 'liberty, equality, fraternity' and the revolts in Europe against the outdated aristocratic and dictatorial governmental systems of the time. The revolutionary ideal was not achieved by the French, and still is an ideal which modern world society has not evolved to embody yet.

Building on the previous foundations laid in Capricorn and earlier, the new political direction should be capable of emerging openly in the West. It will obtain more support and response from the people during this phase, as it will express the main impulses of the Aquarian energy, and be clearly perceived as a positive creative direction to take.

PLUTO IN PISCES (2041–2066)

This is the last sign that Pluto transits through in this cycle. It is a time of endings, a culmination of the whole cycle, and the seed year for the new. The success or failure of the whole transit will be seen and evaluated. What is likely is that the needs of the world, and its hope for the dawning of a New Age, will still be basically unsatisfied, despite considerable improvements and movement towards the achievement of the planetary vision.

These developments will be relatively great, but are likely to emerge mainly from the Western nations, and then spread to the less developed countries of the world. This is because these nations which are facing the problems associated with advanced technological progress, are still having to confront the necessity for global interdependence and the challenges of international transformation and adaptation that it brings. They will be forced by world circumstances to respond to the pressure of the evolutionary current, and to be at the forefront of a movement for international change.

The world situation is likely to be that the modern Western nations are beginning to embrace and embody the new universal and humanitarian values and attitudes, sharing them more equably with developing states, stimulating growth and transformation in those nations it has influence over, whilst these other nations are trying to develop towards the level of society that the West basically achieved by 1900. It is certain that a 'New Age' will not emerge on a world-wide basis yet, but will evolve on a piecemeal basis, as shifts in national attitudes, a growing sense of universal responsibility and common humanity, and in social experiments with new types of government, economic theories, etc. The West is the spearhead of the new evolutionary current, and also stands on the cutting edge of its social impact; it is a difficult challenge to face. Even at this time, the world will still be fragmented. But with the expected emergence of a new, more effective forum of nations, united by the realisation that there is no alternative but to unite in working for a world future, the hope for humanity will be illuminated.

Pisces will bring a time of dreams, looking back into the past, to see what built the present, perhaps to evoke old ways of life, sentimental memories; looking forward into the future, dreaming of the glories to come, the aims to achieve, dreams to satisfy. The world nations will reflect this, as they will reflect the various types of government and conditioning attitudes of the whole cycle; liberal, authoritarian, totalitarian, socialist, dictatorial, 'new age', etc. All of these will still exist in the world, especially in the East and Third World countries. Conflicts could obviously arise from this condition, but the Western nations will have achieved a much deeper unity by now, allied to the USSR and Eastern European states.

Life is but a choice of roads to take; each has to choose the direction for himself, but it is wiser to travel together in brotherhood.

Pluto through the Houses

PLUTO TRANSITING THE 1ST HOUSE

The dominant theme during this transit will be the concern with gaining a greater degree of self-understanding, which is then able to aid in the process of personal integration. You are likely to experience the need for an inner enquiry and search, as you sense the need to evaluate your own nature and life direction almost as a preparation for impending changes and it is likely that whatever degree of success you have at this phase will condition the nature of the following transits.

The tendency will be for you to become more involved with either social, political or religious activities; this can be a more intense continuation of previous interests, or it could be the commencement of a new direction in your life. You will certainly feel a strong urge and impulse within you to become personally identified with the cause that you have adopted as your own; and you will feel that in your personal life you should be a good individual example of the beliefs, principles and attitudes of your chosen cause.

This could create quite a radical change in your lifestyle, as Pluto's energies are designed to undermine any old established order, so that the new can emerge as a replacement for an outworn restrictive pattern of behaviour. This can lead to the sometimes excessive zeal of a new convert, and any such developments need to be guarded against by maintaining a sense of realistic perspective and proportion.

Your whole approach to yourself and life could be permanently changed by Pluto's influence. These changes will be brought about by the synchronicity of external circumstances confronting you with situations and experiences that cause you to feel the need for inner change, allied with a will to accept its inevitability. This may occur as a series of unavoidable experiences which force you towards new environments, as a result of the leaving behind of the old. This can create a feeling that your identity is breaking down if the necessary experiences are initially negative and purgative, as the dissolution of a long-established relationship can serve to shatter existing patterns of behaviour. Alternatively, your identity could be strengthened by involvement with like-minded groups. Whichever is the case, the intent is ultimately the same: to build a deeper, more effective personal integration, to become more fully your own true self.

This will require you to begin expressing your own particular talents and qualities in your pursuit of new ways. This will also involve an inner struggle to become free of those more established and habit-patterned ways of thinking and feeling, so that you can be free to enter into the spirit of the new approach without being pulled back so easily and reverting to the old ways.

You will feel an influx of potent energy into you, and this may create a tendency for you to release this in a destructive manner, attempting to break down any barriers and obstacles that you feel stand in the way of you achieving your new ideals and objectives. Your life will be infused by this energy, and initially you may experience some difficulty in understanding and handling its impact.

It is likely that your awareness of political matters will intensify and deepen, and that you will ally yourself with those political and social groupings that are compatible with your developing beliefs. You should make use of this phase to look for the deeper, underlying causes and values in any political, religious or social context; if you can achieve this, then you will find that your perceptions continue to change and evolve as your understanding and insight is clarified.

You should avoid any tendency to become more ruthless, stubborn and self-righteous in your ideas and in your drive to express them; especially avoiding any temptation to use excessive assertiveness in order to manifest your will, whether it is physical force or mental force through the power of mind manipulation. To offset any such tendencies arising, you should try to unfold those qualities of toleration, co-operation and compassion within the various ways in which you attempt to express the impulse of this transit.

PLUTO TRANSITING THE 2ND HOUSE

Following on from the clarification of the revitalised new direction of the 1st house transit, this main theme is concerned with how you manage to utilise your personal innate talents, qualities and abilities in order to achieve your own goals and ambitions.

You will need to look deeply into yourself, to analyse and evaluate in an honest and realistic manner the nature and potential application of these gifts; and then be prepared to use them in a purposeful direction. Efficiently organised personal management is the key to success.

What you are to look at involves the totality of your life so far; this includes any physical or creative gifts, intellectual accumulation of knowledge and specialist training, your personal philosophy of life and those beliefs and values that you apply in daily living, and your current financial situation and family responsibilities or other commitments. Consider these, and see if you could use them to a better advantage than you currently are doing. Most people have talents and qualities that are under-used due to circumstances, and most are capable of much more than they do actually achieve. This is the challenge facing you during this phase; there will be several ways through which you can achieve more, which will give you a greater sense of fulfilment, provided that you are willing to expend more energy in bringing about this reorientation. The contexts in which this can work involve creativity, devotion to a cause, additional home interests, work, etc.

In a sense, you are asked to 'prove' your capabilities to the world, to openly and clearly demonstrate your own unique individual contribution. For some, this phase indicates that under the influence of a potent ideology as absorbed during a 1st house transit, your personal attitudes held towards possessions could undergo a radical transformation. It is likely that your possessions could either be utilised to support a cause, or be viewed from a totally different perspective to before. Certainly, your attitudes towards materialism will be modified, and now have a different hold on you, perhaps seen in the context of 'stewardship' and less possessively; some could find that their chosen direction is to devote their talents towards greater financial and materialist gains.

It is quite possible that this Pluto transit will aid you by stimulating the inner opening of talents that previously you were unaware of, or were latent and not developed. This could especially occur if the proposed direction is towards either the political or spiritual life. You could discover a sudden flowering of creative talents or qualities that are yours to apply in the 'work' that you have determined to do. In some cases, this can lead to being used as a 'channel' for new impulses to enter society, and to be used in ways which are not immediately recognised by the conscious mind to bring about or influence certain necessary changes in society.

This is a most suitable period for using your talents to the maximum degree possible, in whichever way you choose. Right application of them will certainly bring you greater benefits than you may expect, give you a deeper, more enhanced perspective on yourself, and offer the potential for increased personal satisfaction and fulfilment.

PLUTO TRANSITING THE 3RD HOUSE

During this phase you should demonstrate to others your ability to resolve problems by the application of your intellect, and by those attitudes and values that you have developed and during your life so far. The main challenge which faces you now is in applying them in a practical way.

The more that one can live intelligently in life, whilst remaining true to personal beliefs and principles, the more one will create the foundations of a state of natural inner harmony. As an important aid towards achieving this, it is wise to develop intelligence so that you can become adept at dealing with the world as it is, so primarily what is required is a pragmatic approach based upon a realistic appraisal of life. This is often much more difficult to achieve than is realised; most people fail to deal with the world as it really is, preferring to live with illusions and evasion of reality.

Everyone has to become aware of those 'techniques of living' which seem essential for successful functioning within the society in which we live. Learning the social rules requires years of experimentation, through to the late teenage years, and involves the ability to adapt consciously to the contemporary world. This is a form of pragmatic adaptation, where you have to demonstrate the effectiveness of your individual style of living within the community. One essential 'technique of living' lies in the ability to have good relations with others, and a person can be guided to develop this. Some fail to understand their relationship with society, and become alienated. A future development in education should include more definite social training designed to develop feelings and thoughts of human unity in children.

You may find that a technique of questioning can bring you benefits and help you to grow in understanding, especially when you are not convinced by solutions that others offer to life's problems.

This is because even though you may stimulate a reaction from others, your immediate concern is to discover your own way, the way which is right for you, and this often takes time. Be prepared, though, for others who are also searching to question you in a similar manner; and do not be surprised if they tend to reject your personal way because this is how people learn for themselves, and those who are capable of standing free and independent are always in a minority in life.

What you discover about yourself will prove to be invaluable. It can clarify your life, guide and direct it from within. Hopefully, it will prevent you from wasting time chasing dreams and fancies which you believe will fulfil you in the outer world, because you recognise that lasting fulfilment arises from within.

It could be that this period sees the dissolution of a close relationship with someone with whom you are close, such as a friend, close relative or parent. Perhaps this will occur through death, which turns your thoughts more inwardly upon the quest for meaning in life, and which also serves to sever certain restraints upon your freedom of choice and action. At the least, you will tend to experience the need to move away from those things which bind you, and will search for ways in which you can become more independent.

You could be advised not to become too involved with any extreme ideas at this time, because there is likely to be an attraction to do so, as a reaction to your current situation and as an expression of 'independence'; remember the necessity to 'enquire and challenge'.

Your problem may be that in breaking free of some older ways of thinking, you leap straight into absorbing a new ideology and lifestyle without any discriminative thought, because you experience such a need to feel that you belong somewhere. In fact, the only ones who are capable of free-thinking belong nowhere.

There will be a need for you to be careful in your style of expression, and it will be better if it is not excessively radical at this stage due to any over-enthusiastic reaction to new ideas. Remember that techniques and ways of living should always be capable of re-evaluation at any time. They may stand the test and emerge intact, or they may require adjustments and changes to make them more inclusive and appropriate; they may collapse totally under the pressure of real life. Try not to fall into the trap of being aggressively discerning regarding the ideas of others and challenging them, but choose to treat your own as though they are 'holy script'; in fact, you should be even harsher with your evaluation of your own ideas and beliefs than you should be with others. Using your intelligence in such a way creates a new perspective and sense of proportion, tolerance and understanding.

PLUTO TRANSITING THE 4TH HOUSE

Your main challenge will be to demonstrate your ability to live from a perspective that is grounded within your own personal philosophy in a consistent manner in your daily life; it is an expression of your own unique 'truth'. This is just as likely to reveal to you that you have no real clear conception of your perception of life, and that you may have a need to discover one.

This can involve a re-establishing of the centre of your own unique sense of identity, and it is likely that life's circumstances will create situations that confront you as a 'test'. This will revolve around the concept of 'home'; inner and personal, and your outer home, national and planetary. Following on from the 3rd house transit, you will find that you are having to rely more upon your own resources and abilities, which may also involve changes being made in your personal and home life. As an integral part of this need, you should be taking into account any requirements for your developing social, political or spiritual activities.

You will be attracted towards becoming more associated with those who are expressing plans and ideas for new ways of life for society. Through relating with more like-minded people, you will find that your resolve to live a life more true to your intentions and beliefs will be intensified.

Remember that at this time, you are primarily laying a foundation for what is to come; time and care taken now are of great future importance. You will need to look carefully into the positions you decide to take as 'your truth', paying attention to any current trends in society. Always leave 'space' for new ideas and ways of interpretation to enter, as well as the inevitable impact of life experiences upon any ideology you choose to adopt. Be aware that it is likely to change over time, and that your current enthusiasm may not last, and ensure that you avoid any form of dogmatic approach which would indicate a closed mind. Your 'truth' should change and evolve if it is a living truth, and so should you.

Potentially, one major result of this phase of the process should be a greater inner stability, as you firmly establish your centre from which you will experience the world. It is a multi-faceted world, and any expression which emerges from you should be inclusive in nature, a truth or ideology that in fact can serve to unite people and which encourages them practically to live together in harmony and peace. There are many ideologies in the world which, whilst seeming to preach high virtues, in practice only separate people, leading to political and religious wars; and obviously, this is a way to avoid.

PLUTO TRANSITING THE 5TH HOUSE

This involves the release through Pluto of creative power, offering you the opportunity for enhanced creativity, with the chance to move beyond your current abilities and limitations into new areas of expression. Creativity can be applied in all areas of life, and the personal life can be perceived as an ongoing creative act, as each individual chooses how to build and direct his life.

The main areas of focus during this phase, will include creative self-expression, pleasures and social entertainments, love affairs, speculative ventures, and children. It is a time for 'play' and experimentation through such channels, to experiment in adding new dimensions of enjoyment and in exploring your own nature, learning about new aspects of your own unique individuality.

You may find that you need to control and understand your own emotional drives, motivations and obsessions, as they will tend to attract you towards certain experiences in order for you to satisfy them or confront their nature. Whilst they remain at the unconscious level, you will fail to have a conscious control over your own life, and they can have a negative effect destroying your potential for satisfaction and creativity.

You should avoid any tendency to fulfil your personal drives at a cost to others, especially in your loving relationships or in your career. There is never an appropriate time to move headlong into such activity, especially until you are certain that you truly understand what your real motivations are. Whilst you may be wiser to avoid being ruthless, you may find that the ruthlessness of others has a direct influence on your life.

Pluto has a basic tendency to undermine schemes and intentions, if they are unsuited to fulfilling a more expansive vision and destiny. You may thus find that your creativity is frustrated for some unclear reason, and yet you are expected to continue trying, perhaps through the adoption of a new approach, or by understanding the nature of the direction you are aiming towards, in the light of deeper self-knowledge. If you become involved in new love affairs at this time, they are likely to hold problems in the future for you, and lessons to be learnt. Any ventures in speculative spheres should be carefully looked into before you commit yourself. The key to success lies in the degree to which you can link your new creative endeavours to your level of self-awareness. Unless it is wisely used, this creative aspect of the Pluto energy will stimulate more difficulties in your life; positively used it can move it into new directions and enhance it considerably.

PLUTO TRANSITING THE 6TH HOUSE

This indicates a focus upon the themes of health, employment and service to others.

You are likely to feel attracted towards becoming more personally involved in working to further the aims of some cause in which you believe. You will feel the need to become more committed and active in supporting a particular approach that you believe has the potential to lead to social improvement, to help to resolve a problem area, and to improve the quality of life. This may require that you move through certain personal challenges, which can include disapproval from friends or relatives, unease about your ability to succeed in your endeavours and a fear of failure, a touchiness regarding criticism of your beliefs and doubts over the depth of your own commitment.

It is a period of readjustment, where you are likely to realise that what you feel and think does not match a level of ideal behaviour. You will feel the existence of this 'gap' quite acutely, and this will stimulate you to feel that you should do more, to make progress and move towards embodying your ideals more successfully.

As Pluto provokes an excessive reaction to the area of life which it is influencing, you will have to be careful that you do not display an élitist, divisive and over-fanatical commitment to your special cause. Awareness of such a tendency should lead to a conscious balancing of your involvement. This could move you towards a new form of participation in social activity, and will have the effect of redirecting much of your self-preoccupation towards others. You should find that your insight into people becomes broader and clearer, and gives you additional experience of how the world actually is – although one's view of individuals is usually quite resistant to change. You need to accept this inner impulse, and this is likely to create inner conflict and the pressure of struggle, but it is essential if you are to develop in harmony with the unfolding inner potential.

There may be major changes or disputes in your employment, or you may decide to take a new career/employment direction which more suits your commitment. This can be linked to the activity of social groupings and it is likely that you will be directly affected by reactionary or radical ideologies which are influencing the nature of your work through interference.

If you are basically co-operating with the Pluto energy to bring about personal changes and social involvement, then you will be making positive use of the impulse. You will have to be cautious regarding your health, as illness may occur due to any inner struggle within you, especially friction caused by resistance to change. Illness can often be used as a 'medium' to force change upon a resistant individual, and is symptomatic of adjustments being required in life, internally or externally. Illness can create a 'space' in life, whereby the prospect of reorientation can occur, veiling a hidden opportunity for positive benefits to manifest themselves in the person.

Pluto Transiting the 7th House

Your main focus will be upon your relationship and participation within society, and is likely to involve the development of the 6th house stimulation of involvement with a socially orientated cause. Your attention will be primarily towards what you perceive to be the contemporary problems facing society, and you feel that you have to participate personally in efforts to resolve them satisfactorily for the benefit of all. Your awareness of social reponsibility will be more heightened, and the main challenges before you are those of how best to co-operate with similar thinking people to make a real contribution to social progress. The emphasis within your personal social relationships will be towards those who are in tune with your developing social conscience and ideals, so that your energies are moving towards achieving results founded upon a unity of group purpose. This is likely to be the common ground of your new associates rather than upon any primary friendship qualities. To maintain such shared purpose, self-discipline is often required as well as a commitment to the goal, as friction between personalities is likely at most stages.

In fact, it could be you who is a source of friction, rightly or wrongly. The influence of Pluto upon you can lead to excessive zeal, fanaticism and a totally obsessive concentrated focus upon the cause; so any such tendencies need to be curbed. You may also feel inspired to express a particularly 'purist' view of your understanding, beliefs and ideals; these may be perfectly correct and balanced, and you think that they are, but many would justifiably disagree: 'different strokes for different folks'.

There is likely to be the urge to challenge people on grounds which you are especially knowledgeable about. It offers a sense of personal superiority and confers a feeling of personal validity; yet this tendency can become quite destructive at times. The iconoclastic approach can be most appropriate at the right time, yet few people are ready to have their belief structures shaken, and it is less apt when the hidden intention is to destroy their ideas only to substitute your own in their place. The danger can lie in the fact that they may not be ready to have certain cherished or meaningful beliefs questioned and destroyed; because often each individual has to outgrow them, and if they are not ready then you will be resisted and resented, and division in relationships will occur. Your intentions may well be positive, but such a tendency should be noted, so that more awareness can be applied by you in such situations.

In any sphere of knowlege, there are always different levels of teaching occurring, where the 'truth' at one level can be the 'falsehood' at a higher level; your main responsibility is to realise this fact, and to embody the truth appropriate to your own level to the best of your ability, whilst realising that it may change with greater knowledge and experience.

Any of your relationships are liable to undergo radical change during this phase, although much will depend upon how you handle and express these potent and influential Pluto energies.

You may find that you have to release yourself from any restrictive relationships, in order for you to become free to pursue what you perceive as your 'destiny'. If this becomes inevitable, then try to do so with as much awareness and sensitivity as possible, to prevent others being excessively harmed by any tendency towards an impersonal, ruthless approach which would be self-centred. Sometimes the 'inner calling' to devote oneself towards social change and the good of others, seems to be applied in ways which cause unnecessary pain to immediate families, as though they are not a part of society too.

Pluto Transiting the 8th House

During this phase, you will be preoccupied with the quality of your relationships, perhaps evaluating them in some way, and considering their importance and relevance to your life, and asking whether they are living contacts between the participants rather than superficial connections only maintained by past momentum.

Whilst you will tend to evaluate your relationships from your own personal perspective, needs and objectives, you should ensure that others also benefit from being in relationship with you.

You may need to modify some of the ways in which you express yourself and deal with interpersonal relationships, to enable you to begin building more satisfying contacts. This can involve you ensuring that you are not tending to exploit anyone solely to further your own desires and ambitions; it is easily done, especially at times when you may be concentrated upon your own personal direction, when an intense focus can often lead to a lack of awareness of others and their needs.

You may find that you are attracted towards expanding financial and business interests, especially to take advantage of contemporary business and social trends, or by starting a new business. You will be tempted by opportunities that arise, and become quite enthusiastic about their potential, leading you to be perhaps less cautious than usual. You should be wary of any dubious schemes, and ensure that all is as it seems, as well as being legal and ethical. If you move in such a direction, you should ensure that your attitude towards any such endeavours is suitable and in character, and, ideally, socially responsible, as this will have a strong influence upon any future success.

In several ways, you will find that money will be a dominating theme at this time, and it can easily become a source of disagreement in your domestic life, possibly reaching a point where relationships can break down and a financial rearrangement with partners is required.

As this is a house of regeneration and rebirth, you could experience the unsettling phase when the established foundations of your life begin to collapse; obviously, this can be very disturbing, and painful, but it would be an inevitable and natural consequence of your own choices over the years. If this occurs, it can create a condition in your life which forces you to look towards new directions, especially in relation to partnerships and finances. Take time to see what the lessons and implications of such unwanted changes are, to look honestly at where your own attitudes may have sown seeds of division through a lack of awareness of your partner. For most though, it is more likely that consciously made adjustments in your relationships and finances can lead to beneficial results in your life, and it is an apt time to make them.

If you have an interest and involvement with groups which are associated with the more intangible occult side of life, then this is an appropriate time to deepen your exploration. You are likely to gain valuable insights and new ways of looking at yourself, potentially being reborn like a Phoenix, and creating a firmer sense of direction for the remainder of your life.

PLUTO TRANSITING THE 9TH HOUSE

You are likely to become more interested in matters which concern the intellect and higher mind, and you will be involved in the attempt to understand the basic causes of problems which are confronting modern society. Usually, this implies that you will be seriously applying yourself to some form of disciplined, concentrated study, either to reflect personal interests in such themes and self-exploration, or to pursue additional qualifications of an academic nature. You may also be attracted towards increased travel, as a means of widening your knowledge and experience of life and other cultures.

Potentially, you can develop quite a clear insight and analysis into modern problems, and you may find yourself in a position of advising or leading others towards your ideas of resolution. You may begin to develop a personal concept of a more suitablelifestyle which is more positively appropriate for people, which you then attempt to apply to your own life, and offer to communicate to others. This could lead to a radical change in your life.

Through your studies and insights, you are likely to become more active in opposing certain contemporary attitudes and ideas, those which you believe are not valid or incorrect, and which you try to oppose by presenting your own ideas and beliefs. This could be promoted externally by publicly expressing your thoughts via various media, or it could be mainly internalised as you pass through an inner conflict between your old ideas, beliefs and attitudes and those new ones which are being formulated and emerging from the impact of your inspired new insights. It is likely that you will feel the need to offer something which you believe to be of considerable value to society for it to adopt, as you need to feel that you are making a positive contribution.

You may become quite affected by experiences of hypocrisy and social injustice, and this could be the trigger for the renewal of your search for a greater understanding of society, and of your personal experience and role within it. The style and content of your new outlook, whether expressed to others or experienced within yourself, will be often of a subversive nature, undermining existing established ideas, carrying the quality of being revolutionary in some way, so it is extremely probable that quite radical changes will occur within you during this transit. You will have to guard against becoming too fanatical or obsessive about these new powerful insights, so that you do not try to impose them on others, but carefully and consciously moderate your style of expression to make them more acceptable, and likely to be listened to by others.

Pluto Transiting the 10th House

This involves the issue of power, and the problems related to using any personal or social power in ways which do not abuse or exploit others.

You will still be looking towards making some kind of impact within society as an expression of your beliefs and ideals, so that through your active social participation you succeed in contributing something of meaning and value via an expression of personal power, where the individual alone or within a group can have a distinct influence. This could develop towards your becoming a spokesperson for your affinity group. It involves your attempt to resolve the inner question of 'What can I do to help?' which arises in the minds of all those who become associated with active groups, and involves a sharing of the 'burden'.

Any tendency to be excessive and closed-minded would serve only to distort and eventually destroy those ideals which you originally tried to display; there are many who misapply their ideals in such ways, resulting in an opposite reaction to their initial intention.

If you do emerge into public attention, your social reputation will be directly affected, to your benefit or detriment, the eventual results being influenced by your own actions, choices and decisions.

It is primarily a test of power, whether you can use your influence to further those more impersonal social ideals for the benefit of others, or to satisfy personal desires and ambitions. Certainly you will feel a need to change and reform certain aspects of the world that you live in, and this impulse will affect your immediate social and domestic life.

Your attitudes, beliefs and actions can create both new friends and opponents, and it is likely that you will have to experience considerable criticism and misunderstanding, and that you will appear to some as a controversial figure.

PLUTO TRANSITING THE 11TH HOUSE

The Pluto influence will guide you towards a greater involvement in activities which link you with groups working to create social betterment and change. This will be a continuation and development of those ideals which you have been building, and this is an appropriate time to apply them in direct action.

In making such a choice, it is likely that you are simultaneously reforming several aspects of your personal life and character, as a reflection of the direction that you are taking, by being true to your beliefs and faith in these particular causes. Your aims and ambitions in life may now be radically reversed, and certain aspects could seem unimportant to you now, whilst other values are suddenly extremely meaningful to you; in many ways, you will be like a convert to a cause.

This will mean, too, that your social life is likely to change, and your range of friends and acquaintances will expand or contract, depending on the nature of your chosen path, and how you express it to others. You may need to remember and respect the rights of others and their own freedom of choice, and that what may be right for you at this time may not be right for them, and vice versa. There may be a tendency to express the intense fervour of the new convert, especially if it is your first involvement in social activities designed to stimulate social change, and your enthusiasm may need to be toned down a little; or you may discover that instead of creating enhanced social harmony, you are creating addititional discord between yourself and family and friends. If this is occurring, remain aware of such tendencies, but do not allow them to dominate your social expression, and then you will soon mature and get a workable sense of proportion towards your social involvement.

In all your relationships with others, ensure that your motivations are clear and straight; if you are selfish, then you are likely to experience financial losses and emotional disappointments. Because of the nature of this impulse, and the ways in which you are liable to respond to it, you may need to be careful about your health, and your life at work and home.

Your mind will be opened towards social change and problems, and your perception of these will be changed during this phase, and especially in relation to your own involvement and contribution.

PLUTO TRANSITING THE 12TH HOUSE

This is the final phase in your current cycle of transiting Pluto, and it is a time of culmination and of sowing the seeds for the new cycle. This can be a difficult period, and you are likely to experience inner confusion and a sense of imminent change waiting to happen, as aspects influencing you arising from your unconscious mind will be agitating and trying to rise to the surface of your concious mind. This can be a little strange and disturbing, but allow them to rise, and always accept them, trying to integrate them into the conscious mind. If you try to deny or repress them, then they may cause further trouble until you acknowledge them correctly as aspects to be redeemed and resolved; they can be a major source for deeper personal integration and regenerative power.

You may find it useful to explore certain modern psychological schools of thought (e.g. Jung, Psychosynthesis, Gestalt, etc.), which provide techniques to enable individual wholeness to be achieved. Such an approach can open up new worlds of enquiry and exploration for you, and all are designed to enable you to understand yourself more fully and to enjoy life more.

It is likely that you will have to release certain aspects of the past, in order to make space for the new impulse that is slowly taking shape within you, prior to 'being born'. This will include attitudes, values and beliefs, especially if you find that you are successfully absorbing more of your previously unconscious mind.

You may feel attracted towards becoming more involved in working more directly with socially deprived people, through community aid, etc. This is a sign of your increasing social awareness. You may also experience a higher degree of sensitivity to others' thoughts, feelings and motives, which is caused by the opening up of your unconscious mind. This may tempt you as a result of sensitivity to withdraw more into seclusion and privacy. A technique for protecting your psychic sensitivity could be usefully employed in such a situation. However, it is best for you not to get too preoccupied with your own mental and emotional state, but work through your inner changes whilst engaged in your usual daily life.

CHAPTER 7

The Esoteric Pluto

PLUTO, GOD OF DEATH

IN ESOTERIC OR OCCULT ASTROLOGY, the planet Pluto is associated with the form-shattering force that we know as Death, the ever-present companion and complementary twin to Life, which reflects the apparent world of duality that we generally experience. As an integral lesson and teaching on the occult path, an understanding and personal experience of the 'death process' is essential to any real progress. It is in fact the way towards liberation; the death of the old, and the birth of the new, is the passage towards the promised 'life more abundantly'.

In Western society, death is still a taboo subject, one which most individuals prefer to ignore as much as possible, and it is a fact of life that most find difficult to accept, leading to the majority of people experiencing strong private fears about dying or suffering the loss of loved ones. Despite the West being nominally Christian, with its foundational creed of resurrection and eternal life, apparently most do not have this belief as an effective faith and support when death approaches or intervenes dramatically in their own lives. Underlying this fear is a lifetime of avoiding the inner psychological death process, and the disturbing Christian belief of 'judgement', where the determining of an eternity in a heaven or hell is based upon the conduct of the personal life.

Death is the Great Mystery, a great unknown abyss from which none have ever returned to reveal its secrets – unless one is a believer in reincarnation or spiritualism. Yet it is into this mysterious abyss that the esoteric path leads the curious aspirant, towards a direct encounter with the two poles of human existence, the experience of Life–Death and initiation.

Western society is still basically antagonistic to occultism, magic and mystical explorations, primarily because these ways enter those areas of life that society holds in 'taboo', yet which exert an attracting fascination for many who are able to question those basic social assumptions. There is also the belief that those who search for 'answers' in such directions are potentially socially subversive as their attitudes are not those of the mainstream conditioning. It should be noted, too, that the esoteric path is not normally described as the Path of Death, probably because this would repel many seekers who have not yet received a more accurate understanding of its implications, and so the glamours of the spiritual life are initially presented in a manner calculated to attract, much as the carrot to the donkey. The esoteric path is certainly worth following, and is a key to the ongoing evolution of humanity, and yet I often feel that because the initial presentation of the nature of the path is apparently distorted, many seekers lose their confidence and faith in following it as soon as the way grows difficult and dark. They reach the edge of the abyss, look into the dark emptiness, feel the fear and vertigo rising, and turn away, refusing to accept that this has anything to do with the 'glorious sunbeams and light' spiritual life, and retreat back down the path.

Nobody had informed them how difficult certain stages could be, or what in reality they are likely to encounter. It could be argued that this is a form of selection, that those who turn away are not yet ready, and that those who continue are the only ones capable of experiencing the sequential revelations, and this is probably valid; yet I feel that a truer light should be shining at the early stages of the way, both to inform of the darkness that the seeker will confront, and to reveal the way beyond the abyss, to serve as a support and illuminator.

What is death? What is the influence of Pluto? Walking the early stages of the esoteric path is a progressive experience of dissolution, of releasing all that is acting as a barrier of limitation to the indwelling soul. To the esotericist, death is a passage to life; and to the soul consciousness, what we call life in the world of appearances is but death. Soul consciousness is that level of consciousness where 'nothing is separate', a feeling-experience of unity and oneness, and to 'rise' or 'fall' to that level is a goal of occultists and mystics. Only the death process within life will be considered; it is not proposed to enter into any speculation here as to any after-physical death experiences. Such speculation is not really productive, but a greater insight into the process during life can be useful.

There is a Zen koan mentioned in an earlier chapter, which aptly sums up my attitude: 'If you are not enlightened in this life, then in which life do you propose to be?'

Pluto is the ruler of Scorpio, the traditional sign of death and rebirth, where the old is dissolved at the appointed time or end of its natural cycle. That which is no longer needed, or capable of fulfilling an underlying purpose, is released, in order for a potentially more suitable form to embody the creative seed. From birth, life moves along daily steps towards eventual death, and after the body reaches its destined physical peak of adulthood, commences a progressive downward spiral towards old age and gradual degeneration and loss of full functioning, until the lifelines are severed and physical death occurs.

So identified with our physical forms have we become that this process is hard to accept, especially in the West during our present materialistic period. Strangely enough, our consumer consciousness of perpetual need/desire and ever-replacement by 'new and better models' reflects this natural process at work, and yet is never applied to ourselves! Always the search for newer and more efficient machines to replace outdated models, the changing of houses, clothes, decor, cars, etc. – all makes our society economically viable and embodies an attitude that society tends to condition its members to hold: 'replace through desire, replace through natural degeneration'. Once something has outlived its usefulness, throw it away, get another. Life and natural evolution seems to work on a similar creative principle, one that individually we object to.

The problem is that within consciousness we have separated ourselves from the natural world; we do not really see ourselves as part of Nature – hence mankind's tendency to try to conquer nature's forces – and so resist accepting that we are also part of this creative process which is occurring, that we are a natural flowering of life, a flowering that has a temporary individual lifespan: a natural emergence and a natural decay and disappearance. Certainly, a renewal of natural rhythms and reintegration within consciousness of our essential roots within Nature would be of value to our society, allowing individuals once more to feel an intrinsic interdependence with the world rather than continuing to move towards the alienating, separatist isolation which the contemporary tendency is creating.

The dark face of Pluto is as the God of Death, the destroyer of the restricting form and can be more positively perceived in its capacity as a God of Release. However, such a light-bringing perception is only fully understood by those who have directly encountered the dark face. Entering the black inner abyss is the path to the light, the point of light shining in the darkness. The use of darkness, both inner and outer is traditional in the process of initiation, from the concept of an occult blindness imposed from within on the consciousness of the aspirant, to the use of environmental darkness through which the seeker has to pass to find the light of the hidden chamber in Egyptian mysteries. There, at a crucial point in the seeker's progress through the initiatory labyrinth and pyramidal maze, someone whispers to him in the dark, 'Osiris is a Black God . . .'; which, unless properly understood, is not really what he wants to hear, especially as he believes that Osiris is a God of Light.

Direct spiritual insight, *satori*, enlightenment, *samahdi*, the opening of chakras, or the raising of the kundalini serpent fire, are almost always associated with 'shock' in some way. Initiation through ritual is often based on the principle of creating a heightened state of anticipatory excited consciousness in the initiate (through a variety of techniques, including drugs and alcohol), who is then 'shocked or stunned' into jumping into a new level or dimension of mind by the imparting of some revelation or inner realisation which floods the mind with meaning and comprehension of the hidden secrets, or stops its normal functioning altogether, creating a space in which an inner collapse of illusions and facades occurs.

Pluto destroys all old structures of thought, those worn out and limiting ideas, ideals, beliefs, concepts of self, fading relationships; anything that will repress the destined emergence of the new spirit, new life. He acts like a timekeeper for the perpetual creativity of Earth, reflecting the promise of 'life more abundantly' in a universally impersonal cycle. What is so disturbing about Pluto's impact on people is the inexorability of its influence, the fact that there is really nothing that can be done to oppose the process of disintegration. It is a 'no-win' situation, and to maintain such personal inner supports once Pluto has begun to unravel and dissolve the foundations that they rest upon is to attempt an impossible task. Yet this is what people try to do; there is little awareness in our society concerning natural transformation and change, and so the onslaught of such an inner process is experienced fearfully and as a threat to be fought against, rather than as an inner movement that presages positive growth and a deeper appreciation and experience of life.

Society favours fixedness, stability and predictability; it creates social conditioning to help enforce a social atmosphere and culture of conformity, of limitations on the range of allowable thinking and personal exploration. Whatever society one is born into, from birth and parental conditioning, through school, religious and social programming the individual is restricted to a route which is designed to create a member of society, a preserver of the status quo. We are all the result of this process, and it has both positive and negative results; to some degree, it helps us to live together and to continue the species, yet it also limits personal freedom and inhibits natural inner growth and development, because that leads a person away from the flock mentality, and that is considered to be dangerous to the collective.

Our sense of personal identity is interwined with this conditioning, our national form of emotional and mental programming. Our thoughts, emotions and beliefs are seen as integral to our separate identity; and effectively, we are our thoughts, emotions and beliefs, as we believe that we cannot be stripped free of them without ceasing to exist. Yet is this really the case? To lose all these programmes associated with a personal consciousness is like a death; the death of an old self, and it is precisely this that Pluto attempts to bring about in people. It is also these programmes of separation, of individual/minority beliefs and ideologies that are a major source for most of the problems in the world, the wars fought to support a group belief, social racial problems, religious frictions, the rape of our environment by economic greed. Pluto destroys in order to bring liberation and freedom, and like Lucifer, is a great Lightbringer; we, in the name of freedom, destroy in order to impose our limited separate viewpoint upon the world for self-seeking reasons. The more people we can persuade to hold our opinions and beliefs, then the more proof we have that we are right. The theme of the evangelist and politician. Pluto is anarchic; he frees the person in order to become more real, more themselves, to stand free in their own light. The influence of Pluto terrifies people; confrontation brings death, and it is much easier to escape from the encounter, and to maintain the current conditioning programme. But there is no escape from this god, each day takes everyone nearer to the encounter.

Resisting the natural influence of Pluto, the ongoing change and transformation of fixed self-images, beliefs, ideologies, becomes a struggle, a field of conflict, a repression. We identify ourselves too intimately with personal beliefs and thoughts, finding it virtually impossible to perceive ourselves without reference to roles as husband/wife, parent, worker, member of this political/religious persuasion, etc. When Pluto erodes these from within, stimulating changes through transits and progressions, we panic, and do not know what is occurring or how to deal with it in a creative and positively co-operative way; all we feel is a chill wind of impending death and dissolution of something within that we intimately identify ourselves with. Pluto is a hard and ruthless teacher, and takes no prisoners, and yet through working with that energy, instead of attempting to oppose its process, we find a way to enter into greater life.

PLUTO AND THE SEVEN RAYS SYSTEM

The occult system which is founded upon the concept of seven major energy rays which build and condition the human being and the universe in which he finds himself, was introduced to the West through Madame Blavatsky and the Theosophists after 1875. From the pages of Blavatsky's overshadowed books, *Isis Unveiled* and *The Secret Doctrine*, to the more greatly extended series of books channelled by Alice Bailey under the hierarchical aegis of the Tibetan Master, the Seven Rays occult system has played a central role in the development of the release of ancient mystery school teachings. It is certainly a well-respected and influential source of esoteric information, and the inner contacts from which an occult initiatory path can be followed are still vibrantly active today, welcoming all suitable candidates who may approach them.

The Bailey writings alone comprise over twenty books, so it is not proposed to offer any in-depth analysis of their esoteric wisdom, but it is illuminating to consider the association of the 1st Ray with Pluto.

The 1st Ray is the energy of Will and Power, and is also linked with the traditional sign of death and rebirth, which is Scorpio, ruled by Pluto. The energy of this ray is a great dissolver and destroyer of all manifested forms and species of life at the end of the life cycle, be it on microcosmic or macrocosmic levels of existence, including planets, suns and solar systems.

There are several key concepts which are noticeable characteristics of both Pluto and the 1st Ray, and I feel that the quality of energy which emanates from them is extremely similar when contacted by someone who has a compatible inner responsive structure of body and psyche. These qualities are often compulsive urges, dominating patterns of behaviour inwardly or externally expressed, and include the themes of will and power, authoritarianism, domination, rulership and leadership, desire to control, destruction, disruption, transformation, dissolution of obstacles, and death of limiting thoughts, emotions and forms. These indicate the basic social orientation of Pluto, both in its more potentially damaging and negative expression through self-centred misapplication of the energy, and in its urge to stimulate inner crisis and offer the potential of personal rebirth and resurrection. Every release of power, irrespective of its nature, has both positive and negative effects; so far, we have mainly witnessed its more negative results in the world, but this is but a prelude to seeing its lighted positive face through the planetary vision and individuals who are capable of embodying and using its energy creatively for the good of humanity.

At present, Pluto is the dominating planetary energy in the world, supported strongly by Uranus and Neptune. This is because the transpersonal energy influences affect the soul life rather than that of the personality, and it is the unitive level of consciousness that is being born on earth at present, to act as a directive way forward into the Aquarian Age. These three planets are relatively recent discoveries in astronomy - over the last 200 years - and the esoteric teaching states that until mankind becomes capable of responding to the energies which particular planets symbolise and transmit, they remain undiscovered, as man's ignorance of Pluto until earlier this century implies.

The 1st Ray influence mediated via Pluto cannot be experienced in a positive manner until the receiving individual is walking the 'Path of Discipleship'; basically, it is too powerful to be used correctly by anyone who is not responsive to the 'spiritual soul', serving only to amplify more separatist and self-serving tendencies of power and aggrandisement.

It is only in this century that a stronger potency of 1st Ray energy has been experienced by humanity, since the confirmation of Pluto, and its initial impact was grasped and applied via Germany for a planetary crisis on a world scale. Humanity is approaching a stage in its evolution of becoming a 'world disciple', and many are arriving at the point in their lives of being 'probationary disciples' or at 'the path of trying to find the path', looking for meaning, purpose, understanding and life direction in their inner lives, hence the eruption over the last twenty-five years of a multitude of spiritual ways for seekers.

Pluto is the guardian of the gate of initiation and rules Scorpio, the sign of discipleship, and evokes the appropriate response from those groups of disciples who have evolved enough to be capable of a positive and creative response. As part of their function, they have the task of drawing through this Pluto 1st Ray energy into the mental and emotional levels of humanity, radiating the dissolving energy which is slowly undoing the entrenched crystallised forms of humanity, whilst transmitting a planetary vision that offers a new direction to take.

It is towards the crucial 1st initiation that humanity is being led, the Buddhist 'entering the stream', the esoteric 'birth of the Christ in the cave of the heart'. At this point, the soul consciousness 'breaks through' into the awe-struck conscious mind of the candidate, one-ness is experienced, and the spiritual life becomes a permanent reality for that individual's remaining years of life. It is a powerful awakening, the peak of an energy-expanded consciousness that is the highest the person can undergo at that stage of evolution. It is an entrance into the esoteric world brotherhood of disciples and initiates, all serving as living seeds for the evolution of mankind, anchoring transformative energies within all levels of planetary life.

This 1st initiation is probably the most difficult to achieve for most people, as it is primarily a step into the unknown, a jump into an abyss. A real initiation never ends, but is just the beginning of a new way of life, and is self-evidently undeniable to those who have genuinely experienced the opening of the door; which, like the door in Holman Hunt's painting 'Light of the World', only opens from the inside.

Pluto is associated with functioning in connection with the solar plexus area of the body, which is interesting, as according to the esoteric system of inner energy centres, the 'chakras', the 1st initiation involves the transfer of the energy focus from the solar plexus chakra to that of the heart centre. This transfer of energy into the higher centre corresponds with the initial expansion of consciousness which dissolves limited self-centredness; it is a death of an illusion, that of the separate I-ego-mind, and the individual is reborn (the Hindu 'twice-born') and emerges with an expanded universally oriented state of consciousness, as the intrinsic real nature unfolds and is revealed. The fundamental 'veil' separating the individual and reality and truth is dissolved. This demonstrates the destroyer aspect of Pluto and the 1st Ray, which also destroys death, as it is seen that the human concept is part of the Great Illusion, a figment of the mind's imagination, and that in reality, there is no such thing, apart from the destroying of assumed limitations.

In Alice Bailey's *Esoteric Astrology*, Pluto is described as 'becoming active in the life of the man who is becoming active in the higher sense, his lower nature passes into the smoke and darkness of Pluto, who governs the lesser burning ground, in order that the man may live in truth in the higher land of light'. *At this 1st initiation,the aspirant has to endure the destroying and dissolving power of Pluto, which through inner searching or under the pressure of 'external events' has created a severe self-re-evaluation and stripping down of the personal inner foundations. It is a difficult phase of crisis to pass through, as the process of crystallisation occurs, and Pluto seems to be stirring the unconscious mind violently, and confusion reigns as the contents are attracted into the conscious mind, often creating even more conflict as they clash or demand resolution. The preparatory tension can be extreme, even evoking physical or mental breakdowns, as the crisis of transformation moves closer to its climax, a true turning point in a life, a rebirth of the Phoenix.

The destructive power of the 1st Ray focused through Pluto ushers in change, darkness, death and resurrection, and the resulting transformation is cathartic. At the 1st initiation, the 'arrow of god pierces the heart and death takes place', and 'the Ancient One is no longer seen. He sinks to the depth of the ocean of life; he descends into hell, but the gates of hell hold him not. He, the new and living One leaves below that which has held him down throughout the ages and rises from the depths into the heights, close to the throne of God.'

For the aspirant, the destroying power of death focused through Pluto serves to shatter the dualistic dichotomy of the pairs of opposites, of inner and outer, subjective and objective, of light and dark, good and evil, male and female, death and life. This is the effect of the vision of transcendence, the state of the reconciliation of opposites within consciousness, breaking the age-old human bewitchment.

The continuation of the initiatory path is a progressive maturation of this fundamental enlightenment, and a learning to live with and use correctly the new level of consciousness and energies

This extract and the two below are reprinted with permission from *A Treatise on the Seven Rays, Volume III, Esoteric Astrology*, by Alice Bailey, published by the Lucis Trust.

available to the new initiated disciple. It must always be remembered that the intent of the Pluto energy is only to liberate the indwelling life energy from forms which have become restrictive and inimical to progressive expression of potentiality; the consciousness aspect is never destroyed. The liberated energy then 'awaits' its absorption within newly created suitable forms, where the ability for clearer and effective functioning is possible, similar to the attitude that you do not put new wine in old bottles.

As well as being the ruler (via Scorpio) of the group disciples, Pluto is also the ruler of mass humanity and its creations of society, culture and civilisations. History demonstrates in a vividly clear way the fact that all societies have a cycle of rise and fall, a birth time and a time of dying, and they basically reflect the traditional stages of the individual human life although over a greatly extended period of time. Despite this fact, we never seriously consider that our Western civilisation is also part of this process, and yet we have now entered a phase of transition in the cycle, where a disunited world will fall apart in disarray, but a world directing its efforts towards planetary unity will take a leap into a new future.

The Phoenix quality to Pluto symbolises a triumph over death, where it is a real ending yet truly a new beginning of a new life founded on the ashes of the old. All of the great developments of societies through the ages are subject to this immutable process. From the decline of religions when they become inadequate to vitalise and satisfy the inner spiritual needs of the people; to education which fails to release the creative potential of the people; to the trinity of governance-politics-economics which fails to serve all the people based upon non-inclusive ideologies – all of these socially conditioning forces are liable to degenerate after their point of peak efficiency has been reached, and society begins to disintegrate as these foundations crumble. The old gods die in conflict and crisis, and the result of Ragnarok – as this crisis-point is termed in the Norse myths – is the emergence of the new gods with the vision of the promised land.

The 1st Ray is the impulse of energy for social political direction, and its impact is slowly building towards a new form of politics, and this links with the Pluto emphasis on social involvement, and the whole theme of its direction in the present transit cycle. Even today, there are several international political figures who are reacting to this energy, but unfortunately they are twisting its true purpose in the distorting mirrors of their own minds. It could be said, however, that they are serving as destroyers and agents of separation (despite their own claims), and their real effect is to stimulate others to begin to look more in terms of inclusive unifying and to build a new way. The development and implications of this energy flowing into political channels will be considered in more depth in Chapter 8.

Dane Rudhyar suggests that in the phase when Pluto is nearest to the Earth, and within the orbit of Neptune (1989–1991), a new 'seeding and fertilisation' will occur. Pluto is in Scorpio, and several planets like Venus (esoterically the 'alter-ego' of Earth), Saturn (Teacher, Shadow, Dweller on the Threshold), Uranus (Lightbringer and Illuminator of Mind, Ruler of Aquarius), and Neptune (Mystical visions, Illusions) are gathered together within the sign of Capricorn. As Capricorn is associated with the traditional birthsign of the Christ, and the image of the goat climbing the mountain, there is an indication of some form of impending initiatory activity. The implication is that either during this seeding time, or at some time before the turn of the century, there will be world events of major importance. Whilst this is imminent, the nature of such events and the level at which they occur is likely to be indeterminate. It would be expected, though, that some form of death–rebirth will happen, a confrontation or acknowledgement of humanity's shadow, and a greater degree of light being released as a result in the world; I would expect some physical manifestation of this fertilisation, or physical symbol of its occurrence and implications around this period, but exactly what I would not like to suggest.

A seed has to enter beneath the surface of the earth, gestate in the underworld of darkness, die as a seed, before it can emerge into the light of day as a flower to be seen by all who pass by at the appointed season.

CHAPTER 8

The Challenge of the Transpersonal Vision

IT IS SAID THAT 'WITHOUT A VISION THE PEOPLE PERISH'. The question is, does humanity have a vision, a directing and guiding purpose towards which man is striving? This is a question that needs to be asked of every individual and of the social collective, because within the answer lies the future of humanity.

We are confronting the daunting challenge of a historical crossroads for the contemporary world society. Certainly we cannot stand still at this point, or return back down the road into the past; we have to make a conscious choice which direction to take, which will be the best route into the future. Where, in fact, do we want to go and what sort of ideal world would we want to live in? And what progress can we make for the benefit of future generations, our children and children's children?

It is a time of crisis, a period of decision, a turning point that precedes change. We could continue as we are, refusing to acknowledge that there is an insistent inner demand for change, growth and new directions; struggling to maintain appearances that all is still all right, and that we are still in control and know what we are doing. But if we look around, we can see that there are many problems that we choose to ignore, or postpone dealing with because the challenge of solving them may seem too great or too radical a step to take. The world problem is an amplified version of the individual attitude to difficult areas in life; usually they are ignored as much as possible, hoping that they will pass, thus avoiding the direct encounter with them and the hard work involved in resolving them. They never go away though; they just reappear in another guise, or become more insistent, even to the point of destroying the foundations of a human life if an attitude of avoidance is still persisting.

In the world view of astrology, we are in a crucial period of transition between zodiacal ages, passing on from the Piscean Age into that of Aquarius. Now, as this happens only every 2,000 years or so, none of us currently alive really know what occurs at such times (for instance, at the last changing of an age, Christ emerged onto the world scene and into history) and especially this time when even over the last 200 years, three new planets – Neptune, Uranus and Pluto – have been discovered which reflect extremely powerful energies.

The emergence of Pluto in this century is an important symbol, a herald announcing the end of times and the birth of the new cycle. Two opposite but complementary human reactions to this Pluto penetration into the surface world, are the linking with the power released through atomic fission, and the physical radioactive plutonium that is destructive to humans; and the development of depth psychology as pioneered by Jung and his exploration into the underworld of the human psyche, seeking to heal and integrate conflicting factors.

This appears to be a summation of the challenge facing mankind, the two directions that he has to choose between. The outer direction which can lead to destruction through ignorance and lack of self-understanding, and the inner path leading to healing and self-knowledge, which can then be applied to improve the quality of the collective life. The choice may appear to be obvious, but human nature intent on pursuing its own desires and abrogating social power to unsuitable people can often stumble in many a mess of its own making.

In the West, the traditional way of life that has developed for most of modern society based on exploitative consumerism, capitalism and Judaeo-Christian beliefs and attitudes is showing signs of great strain. Certainly it could survive for some time to come, especially on the momentum that it has established and on the support of people who can conceive little alternative; but the seeds of destruction that have been lying dormant have been greatly stimulated by the arrival of the God Pluto on the scene. The evolutionary current requires releasing and the inhibiting forms and structures that restrict the life of the indwelling spirit and which have been bound within will not be able to contain its power indefinitely.

Historically, cultures, civilisations and societies decline and collapse when the 'inner life' vitalising them is withdrawn to be reborn into new forms. There is no reason to assume that this process will not happen to us, apart from egotistical beliefs. The motivating attitudes and beliefs in the West are unsuitable for the new world that is already present and surrounding us; a new world paradigm is essential. Confronting us is the potential of social disintegration or even worse, nuclear world war, and to survive these dangers requires a collective metanoia, a world change of mind capable of renewing society to avoid the necessity of a social breakdown. How painful this process becomes is really up to us, and perhaps from a pessimistic analysis it looks as though we will make it quite difficult for ourselves.

Throughout the world now, there are the sounds of conflict between the forces of inertia – as often represented by political/social establishments and social traditional attitudes – and those responding to the vibration for evolutionary change; a clashing of ideologies and religious beliefs. The rise of those fundamentalist political and religious reactionary attitudes, looking back into the past for their inspiration, are denying any opportunity for future progress; yet these adherents of the energy of inertia have much social power, much more than those seeking to embody the new approaches at present. Within the collective mind, there is great fear and anxiety at the future we may be creating for ourselves; how can we avoid taking the road to tragedy?

When considering the world at present, the sensitive mind sees mainly a world with no common sense of direction, with opposing national directions clashing on the international stage, and within nations opposing groupings competing to gain power to impose their view upon others. Suffering is common, especially in the Third World countries, though most of it could be alleviated if the world will was united enough, or redirected money into socially beneficial projects instead of into potentially destructive channels. Considerable progress to improve the quality of life for many millions of people could be achieved with current knowledge and technology, especially in those fundamental aspects of civilised living which involve adequate food, shelter, health care, clothing, etc. Yet the world will is not fully aligned with an intention to achieve these aims. Even in most of the countries that are suffering, the ruling élite often seem more interested in buying arms and developing military forces than in feeding their own people.

Through the medium of mass global communication networks, and our television eye upon the world, we can no longer ignore the state of our world. To some degree of accuracy, we have some knowledge of world-wide events on a daily reportage, and so the world has 'shrunk' into being present within our own living rooms. The old state of mind of isolation and world ignorance has been shattered during this century, but attitudes still remain parochial instead of universal. An expansion of the parameters of the human mind is necessary, so that we can come to terms with the revelation of the world that confronts us at the threshold of our consciousness.

The increasing inflow of the Aquarian light into the mind of man is also illuminating the nature and extent of darkness in man and the world; this is why world problems stand in stark relief and clarity, forcing us to consider how best to deal with them. The rising of Pluto offers the energy of transformative rebirth and acts as a stimulus to both negative and positive uses of the powerful energies sweeping into the world mind of earth. Everything is rising to the surface, old patterns, new patterns, repressed tendencies, selfish and selfless attitudes, similar to the process that occurs within the individual who is activating a response from within his own unconscious. If an individual is seeking the light, through meditation for instance, what does he initially find but a rising of his own inner darkness and resistance blocking any progress. We need to remind ourselves that the light is always present, even if our own blindness seems to offer only darkness.

Pluto is acting as a mediator for the new direction of the Aquarian Age, offering a path of world healing and integration to be chosen by humanity, individually and collectively. What is emerging into the world consciousness is a new suitable archetypal vision for a world rebirth, to inaugurate a reorientation of man's mind from dualistic perceptions to those of unity. This is based upon the need for a new, realistic and evocative redefinition of what man is, and what is his relationship to his fellow men, his world and his universe? What is his function and task in life? If the theories of evolutionary progression are valid, towards what purpose is this cycle of body-mind evolving?

We may have developed our intellect sufficiently to break the cohesive binding of the underlying atomic structure, and be dominant enough to impose our will upon a relatively passive environment, but we have little idea of longer-term aims, apart from the amassing of nuclear warheads which we brandish as deterrent threats of mass destruction, or through raping the natural world for short-term profits for a business-rich élite. Is this what we have struggled to evolve towards?

Without a new understanding of man which filters rapidly through into the mainstream society, into education, religion and politics and is correctly absorbed within the culture, we will soon find that our scientific knowledge will lead us ever deeper into areas of social difficulty. The escalation in man's knowledge is increasing so fast that the implications of discoveries are lagging behind, and we are failing to integrate them into consciousness. Even Einstein's work on relativity and quantum physics exploration is basically non-integrated into society at a level of intellect which is accessible to all, because the concepts shake fundamental social precepts and challenge our existing world view. Genetic engineering, through human or animal embryos is rapidly expanding into areas that have great social significance and which can re-emphasise the concept of the 'super-race'.

We have almost the power of gods, the ability to destroy life, to change or mutate species, to manipulate realities and the environment. Yet we lack the essential self-knowledge needed to handle power in a safe and responsible way; we lack an inclusive direction and vision in which such advances can be guided within an evolutionary framework. The social challenge can be clearly seen, the Phoenix vision of Pluto is the emerging light and an attempt at establishing this more clearly on the world consciousness is essential for future security and well-being.

Genetics explores the basic cellular structure of the human form, and one of its findings is quite evocative in that within the source of the cycle of life, unity is the essence. The fertilised ovum is one cell, which then through the process of mitosis, divides repeatedly into creating those billions of human cells that form the body. Each single cell has at its core a pattern of a genetic code which determines the essential nature of form, its pattern of development and its future, as a fulfilment of the original impulse. This genetic pattern is like an archetype of man, present within every human being, containing the whole evolutionary pattern of future unfoldment; an Alpha to Omega state. Similar to the physical brain, which is used to only a fraction of its potential at this current point in time, the genetic code also contains many patterns that are not yet operative in man or at best only partially so in an advanced minority.

Returning to our essence, we see that the archetypal pattern of man is unity, an Alpha point of hidden unconsciousness which is designed to lead to the Omega point of active consciousness. In an existential sense, humanity is 'one' at its heart core, but within the socio-cultural sphere, we are presently in a phase of being 'many', reflecting not the initial unity state or the final unity state of 'one body' but the phase in between of division and many-ness. This is the pattern that exclusive individuality creates of the illusion of separateness. The Zen koan 'If the 10,000 are reduced to the 1, what is the 1 reduced to?' may shed some light on the process.

As we have seen, science is exploring realms where genetic codes and atomic structures are dissolving towards original cause, but what needs to be experienced is the consciousness that is the active explorer, the seeker. It is this human consciousness that can also experience for itself the essential unity of life, the conscious unanimity of the 'one soul', the omega point; to move humanity from the state of disunity and fragmentation towards that of a new 'multi-unity', an underlying unity within apparent diversity to build a new type of collective social life. The influence of Pluto will help to strip us of our illusions, revealing the state that is ever present, yet which is missed through seeing from a false perspective. We need to realise that the truth which is found by biologists in the microcosmic levels of our genetic code patterns is that which is found when the consciousness seeker dives into his own inner depths, those archetypal symbols and patterns of intrinsic unity; and then apply these realisations towards the building of the new universally orientated global civilisation.

In many ways, it is a new resurrection of an ancient pattern seeking to be reborn again in the world, a reformulation of the Ageless Wisdom looking for broader channels to work through. Because it is such a fundamental directive evolutionary pattern, it points a guiding finger towards the highest ideal for humanity, and all real occult brotherhoods are devoted to achieving this omega goal, serving as agents and releasing channels for a unified world view and vision. It can be considered to be utopian, the ancient dream of a Golden Age, a paradise of abundance on earth, and perhaps be dismissed as a forlorn quest for something that we can never find. So why make the effort?

There is a great need in man to dream great dreams, to find ideas and beliefs that offer meaning and purpose to life, to indicate a task, an important function, that all efforts can help to complete – and what is more apt than following a path that is reflected within the essence of his own being? A task which perhaps cannot be completed, but which certainly offers the potential for considerable progress for the planet to be made in the attempt.

One such expression of this emergent planetary vision can be found in this seed statement: 'One God, One World, One Humanity'. This is a potent formula of synthesis and inclusiveness, offering a keystone for the temple of a new culture and civilisation to be born, one which in right expression will indicate an unfoldment of greater maturity for mankind. It is towards the achievement of this that the current and future Pluto cycles are dedicated.

Universal ideas that are embodied in a formula are like living seeds of mind, and can easily become as effective as 'magical words of power' if they become accepted as unifying mental mantric seeds for the feelings and responses of all who resonate to the vision. They can act as vitalised ensouling symbols for a culture, reflecting the direction and order of a future awaiting birth and an underlying archetypal pattern awaiting the time of objective revelation. It is both a herald of the future, yet a reminder of what already exists in the present, and that which has not been recognised in the past.

The period since the Second World War has seen the development of many efforts to build a new global state, to achieve progress in the light of the inclusive seed vision. Success has been varied, but it is clear to all that we must move in that direction or perish. Within the world today, in East and West, there are an increasing number of responsible and socially concerned people who are aware that there is an urgent need to discover a new approach to achieve world peace, freedom and progress which will improve the quality of life for everyone, irrespective of race, colour or creed. Within many groups or none at all, they represent an attitude of heart and mind which recognises that there is a way to live more decently and harmoniously together, and who seek to dissolve those false barriers which separate people from people, nation from nation. The essence of their common vision and intuitive insight is contained within this new universal transcending ideal, which serves as a bridge between different nations and ways of life and ideology. The seed 'One God, One World, One Humanity' clearly indicates a guiding direction for everyone and national leaders to follow through this period of transition and world danger.

The world is in crisis, experiencing labour pains of the birth of a new world society, and those international tensions will lead to immense destruction if we are foolish enough to allow differing ideologies to lead to aggression and conflict. We do not want a stillbirth on our hands after all that effort: we want a healthy delivery for the benefit of all. This vision will help lead the world into the new millennium, progressing from the Communist ideal of universal brotherhood and the democratic ideal of individual rights and freedoms to a new approach which is raised beyond separating ideologies based upon universal attitudes.

'One God' acknowledges the hidden underlying source of life, the intelligent cohesiveness and planned order of the universe. The cosmic Mind/Life which is recognised by the world religions and termed as 'God'. This is not the god of each individual antagonistic religion, but a higher transcendence of all separatist dogmatic self-assertion by each religion as being the only true religion, but where there is the recognition of the unanimity of the one soul of humanity, and the basis of co-operation is found on the common recognition of the spiritual reality of life. This more unitive understanding of 'God' will have space for differing interpretations, but will erode the power of any divisive religions until they collapse. The likely impact will be to dissolve formal religious groupings, being replaced by individual–group associations which are more founded upon personal alignment with this reality within themselves, thus having no dependence upon outer structures and mediating priesthoods.

'One World' is a conscious recognition of the innate interdependence of all life on Earth, the creative fecundity of the life energy which is manifesting itself through a multiplicity of forms in the mineral, plant, animal and human kingdoms. It is a realisation that a suitable ecological awareness and considered action is essential for the well-being of the planet. It is a planetary totality which is joined together in participating in a shared destiny, and which is dependent upon the successful establishment of right relationships between all life, especially by the dominant kingdom of humanity which has the ambiguous power and ability to interfere with the rest of the naturally balanced world. It is also an acceptance that national states and races have to learn how to live together in harmony, and that national barriers are man-made arbitrary creations. A concept of international or planetary citizenship can be developed, where each national, racial and cultural grouping is seen to be capable of making a valid and vital contribution towards enriching a planetary culture of abundance for all, and the unity of life begins to determine international decisions.

Decisions are conditioned by the values and sense of priorities of those in positions of responsibility; what has to be ensured is that those who become elevated to such roles have an enlightened vision of right human relationships and thus can be trusted to perform their function as temporal custodians of the health of the planet. From that perspective, it is seen that the world's resources have been given for the benefit of all life, and that there is ample abundance already available on Earth if wisely conserved and shared. The principle of sharing can develop more equitably, so that resources for food, materials, skills and knowledge can be distributed to areas of need.

'One Humanity' realises that each individual is a unique part of the whole human family, a unique expression of the life energy, and is an essential contributor to a potential planetary brotherhood and sisterhood which is united in a common cause to preserve life and improve its quality for the benefit of all. It is an attitude of mind that seeks to emphasise the importance and value of the individual and all life, in an attempt to aid in the unfoldment of latent qualities within each person and to intensify the evolutionary process. Obviously, there is no conformity of people, and diversity is not to be suppressed but to be encouraged, but on a foundation that has the understanding to use freedom wisely, whereby each is expected to think, act and develop according to his own nature and common sense within a mutually supportive environment. It is an educative process that is designed to lead towards the consciousness of our common humanity which transcends all those past and present separative barriers that are self-created of race, class, ideology, religion, lifestyle, role and sex. We may have to remind ourselves that such barriers are not immutable and immune to change; in fact we perpetually act to re-erect them based on existing patterns of repetitive behaviour. If we so choose, then they can be dismantled over time. Choice can create the new world: '*novus ordo seclorum*', the new order of the ages.

One sphere of potentially radical transformation lies in the realisation that the attitudes and values of each individual which are expressed in daily life are the creative force which conditions the world in which we live. Certain personal choices, which may seem to be of little importance, such as purchasing food or goods from certain countries, can in fact have a major impact on the well-being of people abroad. One current example is the decision made by some not to buy produce from South Africa, in an attempt to place economic pressure on that government to dismantle the laws and attitudes of apartheid.

Rightly or wrongly, individuals are making an economic choice based upon personal values and beliefs to stimulate radical change elsewhere in the world, irrespective of whatever policies their own national governments may have. Awareness of economic interdependence within such people leads to conscious choice in spending their money to help others become freer from imposed restrictions. Collectively, this becomes a creative force which, amplified by the energy of human goodwill, can be extremely potent.

If the attitudes held are primarily bigoted, self-centred and separative through racism, ideology or religion, then we are creating or re-enforcing a world conditioned by fear, hatred, violence and wrong relationships, and the result will be negative, enhancing only suffering. However, if we begin to adopt more creative, constructive and inclusive attitudes, which are based on the necessity and principle of the greatest good for the greatest number, and founded within those inclusive right relationships which are implied by the 'One God, One World, One Humanity' seed vision, then we can contribute towards the building of a better world.

It is a sign of the times that this vision is slowly becoming a motivating guide for many people who are responding to the overshadowing spirit of goodwill, and fortunately there is an ever-growing number of initiatives emerging to help to manifest this planetary vision by those who think and act with a global perspective and whose contagious influence acts as a positive force for good.

'One God, One World, One Humanity' is an archetypal visionary idea, it is a guiding pattern to be drawn through the levels into physical reality, and in fact pre-exists within the unconscious mind at the unitive level. It is a 'seed' which embodies a simple yet extremely profound truth, one which is often overlooked due to the apparent confusion and complexity of the modern world. It has the capacity to carry creative energies to all men and women who seek to be of service in meeting human need. It indicates in a relatively comprehensive but simple way the future direction for humanity to reach global unity, and has the power to transform human attitudes and behaviour, to inspire and motivate individuals and groups to great social achievements. It is a vision that can be shared across the world quite easily in many languages, yet can speak to each in their own tongue and level of understanding, potentially striking a deep resonant chord in everyone.

There are many ways in which we can work with this vision, each in his own unique style according to personal talents, based upon the fact that 'Energy follows Thought'. People can always join together within mind, and use the combined thought-power of many who are motivated by the energy of goodwill to weave this vision deeper into the fabric of the mental life of humanity, thus building an inner reservoir of energy available for the implementation of this vision of planetary unity. In the light of the seed, individual differences do not serve to divide but to enrich, and we all stand as equal participants on a common group meeting ground as human beings on earth. Across national barriers, we can each co-operate with united hearts and minds to create a more positive future. The seed can become a living vibrant 'being', a planetary guide present within all who respond to the vision. Focus thought upon it, consider its implications and direction that it offers for decision-making, meditate with it, share this simple vision with others and see how it can clarify and illuminate the way forward. Most importantly, unfold and discover your own understanding of it, become a lightbringer in the world and live it in your daily lives, let it act as a bridge towards the Phoenix rising of a recreated world.

Endings . . .

TO DISCOVER THE RIGHT APPROACH to an inner relationship with Pluto, it is essential to have a real understanding of the nature of apparently contradictory opposites, to perceive this world of dualistic appearances from the perspective of the apex of the triangle, or the Tao.

Because of the peculiar nature of Pluto, many will instinctively shrink from considering any form of conscious relationship with that planetary energy and would prefer that it had as negligible an influence upon them as possible. But inevitably, this is a way of avoidance, and not an approach to life and the inner process that is supported or recommended in this exploration of the transpersonal Pluto.

From the depths to the heights, from darkness to light, from immersion in the 'objective' world into the inner world of universal mind, from human bestiality to human divinity, these are the paths that Pluto can lead you into, and guide you out from again, but having passed through some form of personal transformation you are never the same again.

To Pluto, everything in life has the potential for transformation; and there is nothing that is considered too unacceptable or 'taboo' to be worked with in a healing and integrative manner. This reflects the broad Tantric attitude on life, which involves a non-judgmental, accepting spirit.

Pluto is the redeemer and refiner of the personal and planetary darkness and negativity, offering us ways that we may choose to take to deal with such problems, and indicating the wisest route to follow for our future on Earth.

The God of the Underworld, one of the many faces of the One God, will treat us quite impersonally, yet can be approached by us as a friend who has our well-being at heart. The future health of our species and our planet lies in our ability to make friends with this power, to co-operate in the universal work of creating light out of darkness.

This is the challenge reverberating in the inner world, to externalise individual and planetary light for the good of all.

Pluto can be a 'dark fate' imposing change on a resistant subject, or he can be a 'lighted destiny' as a co-operative collaborator.

Pluto peers deeply into the hearts and minds of each of us and asks, 'What is your choice . . .?'

Index